PRACTICAL CATECHESIS

A NATIONAL PASTORAL LIFE CENTER BOOK

PRACTICAL CATECHESIS

Visions and Tasks for Catechetical Leaders

JUDITH DUNLAP

ST. ANTHONY MESSENGER PRESS

Cincinnati, Ohio

Nihil Obstat: Rev. Nicholas Lohkamp, O.F.M.
　　　　　Rev. Robert L. Hagedorn

Imprimi Potest: Rev. Fred Link, O.F.M.
　　　　　Provincial

Imprimatur: +Most Rev. Carl K. Moeddel, V.G.
　　　　　Archdiocese of Cincinnati
　　　　　April 2, 2001

The *nihil obstat* and *imprimatur* are a declaration that a book is considered to be free from doctrinal or moral error. It is not implied that those who have granted the *nihil obstat* and *imprimatur* agree with the contents, opinions or statements expressed.

Cover design by Mike Winegardner
Interior design by Sandy L. Digman
Electronic pagination and format by Sandy L. Digman

ISBN 0-86716-463-8

Contents

Editor's Comment

I t is a daunting task to write regularly and well about religious education, a wide and varied field undergoing enormous change and intense scrutiny by critics on all sides. In some parishes religious education encompasses sacramental preparation for adults and children; family programming; weekly instruction; recruiting, training and nurturing of volunteer catechists; inviting, evangelizing and catechizing parents; planning Liturgy of the Word with children; youth ministry; working with persons physically and mentally disabled; small faith communities; and serving as a liaison between all those in religious education and the parish at large. Whew!

Yet Judith Dunlap, experienced in chaos as the mother of five children, has calmly touched on each of these with personal warmth, humor and a sure hand.

Readers benefit from her ability to speak as a parent, sharing the heartwarming episodes from her own family life that have given particular appeal to her column in CHURCH magazine for nearly a decade. It is she who taught us editors to write of "parent(s)" since so many children have but one. Not surprisingly, Judith has developed something of a following.

Readers of this book gain much from Judith's experience in markedly different types of parishes—affluent, middle-class and racially mixed—and the wealth of practical suggestions she includes, already parish-tested. She draws on the work of the Catechetical Renewal Network and the National Parish Coordinators and Directors and the writings of the U.S. Catholic bishops. She explains how to apply the principles set out in the *General Directory for Catechesis*, making that document spring to life.

Readers will also find in these pages Judith's own elucidation of several major ideas reflecting the direction parish religious education is taking today. I have taken the liberty of summarizing them:

Catechesis includes much more than religious instruction; it is really about ongoing conversion and faith formation; as such it ought to enliven, activate and make conscious each person's faith.

The best parish catechesis takes a pastoral approach, welcoming people of all ages; helping them to form relationships in the parish; and involving them in parish life—its worship and sacraments, its social life or community, and its mission/outreach.

Catechesis is developmental; it takes place in stages over time; it must respect the developmental stage of each person, beginning with pre-evangelization or evangelization even for adults, for example, if that stage applies.

Catechesis must include the basics, such as the language of faith, the mysteries celebrated in the liturgy, the Church's social and moral teachings and history.

Catechists do not and cannot "give" children faith; rather, catechists help them to discover and develop their faith in their encounter with the worshiping community and with God.

In handing on the faith to children, the role of the parent(s) is primary; the parent(s) lay the foundation and form the infrastructure of a child's faith life; hence parishes should do all they can to support parents, by holding regular meetings of parents and teachers; seizing opportunities to evangelize parents at such "teachable moments" as the children's Baptism, first Communion, and Confirmation; helping parents to share their faith with their own children at home; providing adult catechesis in the parish so that the faith of parents (along with that of all other adults) keeps growing; and by finding ways to help parents in the parish build networks with each other.

Catechesis in parishes can take many forms other than (or in addition to) formal classroom instruction. Alternative forms are currently being tried in parishes. Examples include:

—family-centered catechesis in which intergenerational groups meet in homes or at the parish for prayer, a Scripture lesson, activities and service projects;

—neighborhood clusters where lessons and activities are carried out in homes, after the "teacher" has prepared the lesson with the guidance of the parish DRE;

—summer Vacation Bible Schools.

If you have picked up this little volume hoping for the basics, you will surely find them and much, much more.

Karen Sue Smith
Editor, *CHURCH* magazine

Preface

"A vision without a task is a dream. A task without a vision is drudgery. A vision and a task is the hope of the world." This proverb, found in a church in Sussex, England, circa 1730, hangs in my office. It speaks a truth I am familiar with. In more than twenty years of parish work I have certainly spent enough time dreaming visions and grumbling about why they did not happen. Along with most catechists I have experienced the drudgery associated with seemingly endless tasks. But throughout those years I was also blessed to be a part of several groups and planning teams that matched appropriate tasks with attainable visions and made good things happen. The chapters that follow share some of those successes.

For this book I collected and revised and updated columns I wrote for *CHURCH* magazine from 1993 to the spring of 2000. *Practical Catechesis* reflects not only my own viewpoint that catechesis is a matter of heart as well as head (formational as well as instructional), but also offers some practical ways of making that kind of catechesis happen.

As I reread the material I realized that both the Church and I have changed since I began writing. When I wrote my first article, four of our five children were still living at home. Now ten years and four grandchildren later my husband and I are enjoying an empty nest. The Church, experiencing the "graying" of her own members and possibly also worried about an emptying nest syndrome, has named evangelization a top priority for catechesis. Parishes are realizing the need not only to reach out to new people but to be more deliberate in nurturing their own. To accomplish this, Church leaders are suggesting that the baptismal catechumenate, a formational rather than an educational model, serve as the inspiration for all catechesis. I was pleased as I read over some of the older pieces in this collection to realize that my colleagues and I have been working out of this "new" mind-frame for years.

My own concern for the state of catechesis began almost twenty years ago when my children began attending the parish religious education program. It was also my first year working as a director of religious education at a parish committed to total catechesis. On staff were a full-time adult education director and a liturgist who worked together to initiate the new Rite of Christian Initiation for Adults. Since I was a part of the team I was able to observe the success of this formational approach and adapt the concepts for our parish's children and teens.

With the help of some dedicated volunteers we designed programs and processes that involved our young people in the spiritual, social and service aspects of parish life. We had two objectives: to build strong peer communities and to make our youngsters feel they were welcomed and that they belonged to the larger parish community. Through the years many of the ideas and approaches we incorporated were shared in my columns.

As you read this book you may notice that family catechesis has always been a priority for me. I know its value on a personal as well as a professional level. For ten years my own family participated in a program I facilitated at our home parish. Like so many of my colleagues I believe that the family is crucial in the faith life of all of its members, adults as well as children. Parish catechetical leaders have a responsibility to assist families in this vital role by offering resources as well as opportunities for families to network and support each other.

Throughout this book you will discover various catechetical approaches alternative to the classroom model. My own interest in alternative models of religious education began in 1984 when the professional organization to which I belonged processed the results of Dr. Tom Walters's survey, which we had just completed. One of the questions on the survey was "How effective is the present classroom model (one to one-and-a-half hours a week) for religious education?" Fifty-one percent of the directors of religious education in our archdiocese thought the classroom model was either basically or totally ineffective.

This revelation prompted about a dozen of us to form a task force to find alternative models. The group met for fifteen years and in 1991 became a part of the national Catechetical Renewal Network. I am much in debt to the members of both groups, local and national, for the thoughts and ideas they shared with me. The professional organization of religious educators in Dayton and Cincinnati continues to meet monthly for support and to share resources. The people involved in catechesis in the Archdiocese of Cincinnati are an extraordinary group. I am grateful to all of them for sharing their wisdom over the years and allowing me to pass it on to you.

Two people in the catechetical world have served as mentors and models for me: Dr. Françoise Darcy-Berube took me under her gentle wing years ago, offering hope and encouragement both professionally and personally. Dr. Tom Walters kept me grounded, working toward realistic expectations and objectives. Both shared freely and often their wisdom and experience, ready to answer a question or help me sort out my thoughts.

Many others also deserve my gratitude. Karen Sue Smith, editor of CHURCH, provided not only superior editing skills but also consistent encouragement and support. The National Pastoral Life Center introduced me to the catechetical speaking circuit. Many people across the country allowed me to share their creative ideas. Since speaking comes much easier to me than writing, I am most grateful to my husband Roger, who has read first, second and third drafts for over ten years and helped me get from point A to point D without skipping anything in between.

The content of *Practical Catechesis* is the result of the unselfish generosity of many people who helped shape my ideas and assisted in giving them form and structure. Catechesis at its best follows this same process. It takes the unselfish efforts of community—both family and parish—to help shape and form the faith of each member. Parish catechetical leaders have the privilege of facilitating that sharing of faith. My hope is that this book offers some ideas and practical help for you to accomplish this.

Judith Dunlap
May 2001

Foreword

Many things are unusual and remarkable about this book. The first, of course, is its author.

What is unique about Judith is that she not only has the intellectual formation of a master's degree in theology but she has a firsthand experience of almost all forms of catechetical ministry, both personally and professionally.

Her own family life with her husband Roger and their five children was an extraordinary "laboratory," offering the perfect stage for experimenting with various types of family Christian education.

But because both Roger and Judith are such dedicated and creative persons, they got involved over the years in a great variety of catechetical ministries in the different settings and parishes where they lived. It was an amazingly rich and diverse experience from which developed a wealth of insights, convictions and practical skills that allowed Judith to become the great catechetical leader she is today.

When I first met Judith at a convention where Bob Humphrey, from the New York Conference of Diocesan Directors, was trying to organize an alternative catechetical network with a few pioneering spirits, I was struck right away by the richness of her personality and of her experience, as well as her simple, unpretentious approach to people and by her pragmatic way of tackling problems, notwithstanding her warm personal charm. From that time on we kept in touch and I was always enriched by our contacts over the years.

Judith was blessed, of course, to be part of what she calls "the extraordinary people" of the Cincinnati archdiocese religious education community. As she writes in her preface to this volume, a dozen of these dynamic people formed a task force that met regularly for fifteen years. They were instrumental in transforming the newborn Alternative Model Network into the well-known Catechetical Renewal Network, which Judith chaired with skill and generosity for many years, along with a few other dedicated people.

Another unusual aspect of this book is its wide range, indicative of Judith's sense of the importance and relevance over the years of an ever-widening range of topics. This characteristic offers an interesting glimpse of the evolution of catechesis in the country during that time.

But the book also allows us to see how Judith herself evolved through more than thirty years of her ministry as a parent and a professional catechist. We discover how she accepted being challenged by new questions or problems, how she dared to initiate new things, how she learned from her mistakes (as in the delightful story about Rena in the youth ministry chapter in Part Four).

Catechists and directors of religious education will feel encouraged by someone who understands so well the complexities of their tasks, but also challenges them to grow and become more creative through the difficulties they face daily. Parents will be delighted with her family memories and be encouraged by her profound conviction concerning their irreplaceable role in the religious awakening and formation of their children. Both professional educators and parents will be confirmed in their conviction about the tremendous importance of networking among themselves to offer each other the support and friendship we all need if we are to live a Christian life in our troubled and changing world.

If in this book you look for a systematic presentation of what catechetics is about, you will be disappointed. But if you look for what real-life, hands-on catechesis is about, you will be fulfilled. You will find yourself revitalized, refreshed and stimulated on your journey.

This book is truly a treasure chest for parents and catechists. Don't read it in one shot, just enjoy the chapters, one at a time, according to your present needs and concerns. They will make you think, smile and rejoice that, indeed, when we try to work together with courage and imagination in the freedom of the Spirit, wonderful things can happen.

Françoise Darcy-Berube

Part One
Visions and Tasks

Introduction

*Other seed fell into good soil and brought forth grain,
growing up and increasing, and yielding thirty and sixty
and a hundredfold.* —Mark 4:8

The parable of the seed and the sower (Mark 4:3-8) is the first
scriptural reference cited in the *General Directory for
Catechesis (GDC)* and offers a superb vision for the ministry of
catechesis. We know that the seed is the word of God, and the
sower is Jesus Christ, alive two thousand years ago in Palestine
and today in his Church (*GDC* #15). As Church we are called to
continue sowing the seed by proclaiming through voice and
action the word of God. As catechists within that Church we are
also charged with the task of preparing the soil to receive the
word. It is our job not only to proclaim the word but also to create an environment for the seed to take root and multiply a hundredfold.

Each parish and every catechetical leader is different. The
General Directory offers us a vision; if the vision is going to be
more than a dream we have to set about the task of applying it
to our own situations. In the chapters that follow you will find
suggestions and ideas to help make those applications and to
concretize the tasks.

In the first chapter of Part One we look at how the *General
Directory* continues to develop the vision. The second and third
chapters suggest ways that the parish and the catechetical
leader can help to make this vision a reality. One particular
approach is offered in the fourth chapter, "Setting Up a Parish
Video Library." In the last chapter of Part One we look at five

different expressions of the vision and name the tasks that will help them come to be. Throughout the rest of the book, the vision continues to be highlighted as various approaches and ideas are offered to give the vision form.

CHAPTER ONE

The *General Directory for Catechesis:* Just a Taste

I began my studies in theology in the mid-seventies, about the same time the national catechetical directory for Catholics of the United States was being put together. That publication, the bishops' pastoral letter, *To Teach As Jesus Did*, and the *General Catechetical Directory* (known by the initials, *DCG*, and published in 1971), were the primary texts used in the courses I took. The most significant aspect of those documents for me, as for so many others, has been the four key elements of catechesis: message, community, service and worship.

Message, Community, Service, Worship

Those four words, which I took in like a mantra, helped center catechesis; catechesis is more than just religious instruction, textbooks and classrooms. While we are still struggling to integrate those four interlocking dimensions of catechesis in our parishes, some progress has certainly been made. Parish renewal programs, small faith communities, family catechesis and Liturgy of the Word for children are only a few of the fruits of that effort. Now we have the new revised *General Directory for Catechesis* from Rome, published in 1997, with its strong emphasis on evangelization and catechumenate catechesis to challenge us even further as we begin a new millennium.

The English translation of the *General Directory for Catechesis* became available in January 1998. The revised *Directory* is more than twice as long as its predecessor. It rambles a bit, uses exclusive language and is often repetitious. Still, much can be said for the theological and pastoral direction it takes. By design, the original inspiration and content of the 1971 publication are respected, and the new *Directory* keeps the same basic structure. Two things, however, stand out: the situation of catechesis in the context of evangelization and the strong emphasis on initiatory catechesis. These set the ministry of religious education or faith formation in a much broader arena, which could offer interesting directions for catechesis in this new century.

The new *Directory* consists of five parts, plus a preface, introduction and conclusion. The preface makes clear that a number of publications and assemblies helped to shape the revised edition, but three played significant roles in the finished document—*Evangelii nuntiandi (EN)*, the *Rite of Christian Initiation of Adults* (RCIA) and the *Catechism of the Catholic Church (CCC)*. The first two resources are foundational to Part One of the *Directory*. The catechism is a primary focal point of Part Two, "The Gospel Message." Part Three deals with "The Pedagogy of Faith"; Part Four with "Those to be Catechized"; and Part Five, "Catechesis in the Particular Church."

You can find a summary of what is in the document by reading the table of contents. What I offer here is a rather simple thematic synopsis of Part One, choosing some of the general topics I find particularly helpful, probably because the ideas covered are ideas that many of us in catechetics have been discussing for years. It is encouraging to discover the Church's magisterium in agreement with the experience of those ministering in the field. Along with the summary, I present a sample to give you a bit of the flavor of the document. I hope it will give you an appetite for reading the whole *Directory* yourself, if you have not already done so.

Part One: 'Catechesis in the Church's Mission of Evangelization'

Catechesis is rooted in God's own self-revelation. God, the source of all life, chose to be revealed in both word and deed using "human events and words to communicate his plan; he does so progressively and in stages (CCC 54-64), so as to draw even closer to man" (*GDC* #38). Divine Revelation reached fulfillment in Jesus Christ and is transmitted to the world by the Church through the work of the Holy Spirit (*GDC* #38-45). As such, God is both the source of our faith and the model of the pedagogy of the faith. (See *GDC*, Chapter One of Part Three, for more.)

Word and deed also bring about evangelization, the work of transmitting revelation to the world. While evangelization is certainly about proclaiming the word, it is more than knocking on doors and preaching on street corners or television. It is celebrating the mystery in ritual. It is living the word in service and mission (*GDC* #39). "The Church 'exists in order to evangelize'[1]... (*EN* 14) Proclamation, witness, teaching, sacraments, love of neighbor: all of these aspects are the means by which the Gospel is transmitted and they constitute the essential elements of evangelization itself" (*GDC* #46).

The objective of evangelization is conversion. It is life-altering and involves the whole person. The fruits of evangelization are not a one-time decision but, rather, a lifetime commitment to ongoing conversion.

Three Scenarios for Evangelization

Today's world of socio-religious diversity offers three basic scenarios for evangelization and catechesis (*GDC* #58). Each requires a different and precise response. In the first situation, Christ and his gospel are not known or there is no Christian community mature or strong enough to live out the faith. In this situation, catechesis is usually developed within the baptismal catechumenate and directed primarily to young people and adults.

The second situation involves Christian communities with solid ecclesial structures, fervent in faith and Christian life, who live the gospel and are committed to the "universal mission." In this case the community itself, through its pastoral activity, offers a living witness to the word, evangelizing and catechizing. Children and adolescents are also nurtured through a variety of processes leading to Christian initiation. Adults in these situations also need different types of Christian formation.

The third scenario is an intermediate situation in which entire groups of the baptized have either lost a living sense of the faith or their faith seems to be a purely exterior reality. This situation requires a "new evangelization" involving precatechesis. This precatechumenate formation will, it is hoped, lead to true, interior conversion.

Initiatory Catechesis

Initiatory catechesis plays a part in all three of these situations. In initiatory catechesis religious instruction is limited to the fundamental essentials of faith. There is no need to present the whole catechism. Christian fellowship, sharing faith stories, celebrating rituals, praying and serving together are equally important. Indeed, the *Directory* reminds local churches that the model for all catechesis is the baptismal catechumenate. The structure *per se* need not be slavishly copied (particularly in post-baptismal catechesis). Rather, the gradual nature of the process, the essential role of the community, the rich use of symbols and rituals, and most especially the spirit and dynamism of the baptismal catechumenate serve as an inspiration to all other catechetical efforts (*GDC* #59, 88-91).

"In proclaiming the Good News of Revelation to the world, evangelization invites men and women to conversion and faith.... The Christian faith is above all, conversion to Jesus Christ...full and sincere adherence to his person and the decision to walk in his footsteps.... This demands a permanent commitment to think like him, to judge like him and to live as he lived..." (*GDC* #53).

"Frequently, many who present themselves for catechesis truly require conversion. Because of this the Church usually desires that the first step in the catechetical process be dedicated to ensuring conversion...[this] 'new evangelization'...is based on the precatechumenate.... Only by starting with conversion...can catechesis, strictly speaking, fulfill its proper task of education in the faith" (*GDC* #62).

"Catechesis acquires certain characteristics in virtue of

being an 'essential moment' in the process of evangelization...
[initiatory catechesis] is a comprehensive and systematic formation in the faith...this comprehensive formation includes
more than instruction: (it) is an apprenticeship of the entire
Christian life...a basic and essential formation...centered on what
constitutes the nucleus of Christian experience, the most fundamental certainties of faith and the most essential evangelical
values" (*GDC* #67).

In summary, initiatory catechesis not only comprises but
surpasses mere instruction. It is not a theological investigation.
Rather, "it incorporates into a community, which lives, celebrates and bears witness to the faith" (*GDC* #68).

Continuing Catechesis

Ministering to the baptized faithful in continuing catechesis
also involves much more than religious instruction. In this
ongoing catechesis the community plays an even more significant role, affirming and challenging an individual's faith. In the
process that individual faith develops an even stronger tie to
the Christian community. Faith is nurtured and sustained not
only through the gospel but also in the Eucharist. Both the individual and the community's faith are formed through word and
ritual. Both are empowered by the Holy Spirit to live out that
faith in service to each other and the larger community, carrying on the missionary activity of the Church (*GDC* #69-70).

The document suggests various forms of continuing catechesis: Scripture study and reflection, study of the social teachings of the Church, liturgical catechesis, spiritual formation,
practical catechesis that is relevant to an individual's lifestyle
and, finally, theological instruction. The *Directory* suggests that
theological instructions serve as a systematic means of deepen-
ing the Christian message and that "in a certain sense, it is
appropriate to call such instructions 'perfective catechesis'"
(*GDC* #71).

The Objective and the Six Fundamental Tasks

The final chapter of Part One of the *Directory* deals with the objective and the six fundamental tasks of catechesis. The objective takes us back to where we began, that is, a deeply personal conversion lived out in community and mission. "The definitive aim of catechesis is to put people not only in touch, but also in communion and intimacy, with Jesus Christ" (*Catechesi tradendae [CT] 5; GDC #80*). "Communion with Jesus Christ, by its own dynamic, leads the disciple to unite himself with everything with which Jesus Christ himself was profoundly united: with God his Father, who sent him into the world, and with the Holy Spirit, who impelled his mission; with the Church, his body, for which he gave himself up, with mankind and with his brothers whose lot he wished to share" (*GDC #81*).

The *Directory* spells out the six tasks: knowledge of the faith, liturgical education, moral formation, teaching to pray, education for community life and missionary initiation (*GDC #85-86*). The *Directory* goes on to explain that all six are necessary; omitting any one of them limits the full development of Christian faith. Each in its own way realizes the objective of catechesis, yet all six are totally interdependent. The *Directory* reminds us of the need for maintaining a balance between head and heart, knowledge and experience, word and ritual, in naming the two principle means of fulfilling the tasks of catechesis: transmission of the gospel message and experience of Christian life. Finally, the *Directory* states that every dimension of faith must be rooted in human experience (*GDC #87*).

Adult Catechesis

Finally, while children and adolescents will always be a concern of the Christian community, the basic thrust of the *Directory* implies that adults are the primary focus of catechesis. "Catechesis for adults, since it deals with persons who are capable of an adherence that is fully responsible, must be considered the chief form of catechesis. All of the other forms which are indeed always necessary are in some way oriented to it" (*DCG* [1971] 20; *CT* 43; cf. Part Four, Chapter II).

Message, Community, Service, Worship

We continue to work with this new tool toward integration in our parish catechesis of message, community, service and worship. It is apparent after reading the *General Directory* that parish catechesis in the future will mean an integration of all ministries preparing, nurturing and celebrating the faith life of parishioners, young and old.

---

[1] In this as well as in other excerpts from the *General Directory for Catechesis*, extensive notes may be found in the original.

CHAPTER TWO

Evaluating Parish Faith Formation

W hen I first began working in a parish, most catechetical leaders in our archdiocese were called directors of religious education, DREs for short. Today, many years later, when I scroll down parish listings, I find a variety of titles. More and more parish catechetical leaders are called directors of faith formation or ministers of faith development. The change in title reflects today's broader vision of catechesis, a vision confirmed in the *General Directory*.

More Than Religious Education

This vision reflects the understanding that catechesis is more than religious education. It is more than learning *about* one's faith. The aim of catechesis is to help people grow closer to God, "to put people not only in touch, but also in communion and intimacy, with Jesus Christ" (*CT* 5; *GDC* #80). Catechesis is about ongoing conversion. Such conversion demands a commitment to think like Jesus, to judge like Jesus and to live as Jesus lived (*GDC* #53). Catechesis is about faith formation.

We have been preaching for years that faith is not just a Sunday morning activity. We know that a lived faith is an integral part of a person's life. It is as much a part of who a person is as DNA. Faith formation in a parish's life is similar. It is not just a Monday evening class or something that happens every other Tuesday when the youth group meets. A person's faith is being formed in and through every parish function—at Lenten devotions, at community outreach, at parish celebrations and festivals, even at finance meetings. Faith is formed most especially when Christians come together with other Christians for Sunday Eucharist.

The *General Directory* offers a wonderful opportunity for parishes to look at how well they are engaging their members, young and old, in the process of faith formation. Since catechesis is seen as the responsibility of the entire Christian community (*GDC* #220, 221), and the particular responsibility of the priest (*GDC* #224, 225), such evaluation and planning should be conducted by the whole parish staff. With a little adjustment, evaluation can also be done with the parish council or in a town hall setting involving the whole parish.

Evaluating Parish Faith Formation

If your staff or council is willing, take some time together to reflect on who you are as a parish and how you live out your catechetical mission. What follows is a suggested meeting format, which you can adapt or change to suit your needs. As you read it, you may want to make some notes about advance preparations required, such as reading over the portions from the *Directory* yourself and having copies on hand for others to refer to. Be sure to pass this article along to all the appropriate persons in the parish who would be involved in planning such an evaluation.

The process. Start with prayer and Scripture, reading Mark 4:3-8, the parable of the sower and the seeds. Then quote the *Directory*'s definition of *the particular church*, "a community of Christ's disciples...who live incarnated in a definite socio-cultural space" (*GDC* #217). While the "particular church" in the *Directory* refers to a diocese, the definition also holds true for parishes. *(This definition will be taken up in more detail later in the meeting.)*

Define terms. Ask participants to write what they think the words "community" and "disciple" mean. When they have finished, ask them to discuss their responses. You might be surprised at the diversity of answers. Print the following two descriptions for each participant and allow time at the meeting to read them. Ask for comments and observations of how these descriptions compare to their own:

Community. A community allows for diversity and differences, even disagreements. The *Directory* tells us Jesus' teaching calls for catechesis to inculcate certain attitudes of community life, "the spirit of simplicity and humility...." (Matthew 18:3); solicitude for the least among the brethren... (Matthew 18:6); particular care for those that are alienated... (Matthew 18:12); fraternal correction... (Matthew 18:19); mutual forgiveness... (Matthew 18:22). Community relationships are summed up in John 13:34, "love one another as I have loved you" (cf. *GDC* #86). Christian communities are to live, celebrate and bear witness to faith; and to welcome and support each other, particularly those who are being initiated (*GDC* #68,69).

Disciple. A disciple is not only a follower but a learner, an apprentice who models herself on the master. This is an active not passive role. A disciple is someone who learns by watching, listening, doing and redoing. Disciples learn by hearing and seeing the gospel proclaimed and by experiencing Christian life (*GDC* #87). Disciples are involved in "an apprenticeship of the entire Christian life...which promotes an authentic following of Christ" (*GDC* #67).

Affirm ministries. Ask parish staff or council members to consider the various ministries represented by the people present. Ask everyone to write one positive example of how each ministry has developed or demonstrated community or discipleship. Share these affirmations.

Plant seeds. Reread aloud the opening Scripture reading, Mark 4:3-8. Explain that it is cited as a prelude to the introduction of the *Directory*. The *Directory* goes on to tell us that the seed is the word of God and the sower is Jesus Christ. Today, Jesus is present through and in the Church. The Church, and within it the parish, becomes the sower (*GDC* #15, 16). If the seed is going to take root, parish ministers need to be aware of the ground in which they are planting. They need to be willing to prepare the soil and do some tilling and weeding. And they need to know that planting and nurturing the word of God are part of every parish ministry.

Know the ground. Reread the definition of the "particular church." Explain that socio-cultural space means the social and cultural makeup of the parish itself, as well as the larger encompassing society (culture) within which the parish finds itself. Ask each staff or council member to jot down the various diverse groupings within your parish. Some suggestions from the following might be given: age, culture or ethnic background, physically or mentally challenged condition, family status, parochial school students/parents and so on. (The thematic index at the back of the *Directory* will give you references to most of the above listings.) Share lists, recording them on newsprint or a board visible to all.

Prepare the soil. Make a list of some of the ways Christian community is already being celebrated within and between the groups listed. Ask each person to think of examples within their own ministry as well as in other areas of parish life. Share responses, using a colored marker to check each group mentioned. Draw a red line connecting groups that celebrate community together. Brainstorm ways the parish can be more deliberate in building community within and between the groups listed, particularly groups that have *not* been checked. Mention that practicalities will be addressed later, that this is time for generating ideas for building genuine community.

Follow the same process regarding discipleship. Make a list of ways the gospel is being proclaimed through word or action with and within each parish ministry. In what ways are people being given opportunities to learn, share or practice their faith? Are prayer and Scripture a part of your gatherings and meetings? Are participants encouraged to reflect on the readings, to apply the Scripture to their own lives, to ask questions, to share insights? How does every committee, every ministry, apply itself to the basic gospel priority of reaching out to those in need? Again share responses, marking groups mentioned with a different colored marker. Brainstorm ways the parish can be more deliberate in helping people live out their apprenticeship in the faith (discipleship) with, within and between the diverse groups listed on the newsprint.

Till and weed. Choose one or two particular groups on which to focus. For example, ask how can we help to build community among those involved in our parochial school and our parish program of religious education? Or, how can we make Sunday liturgy an even greater opportunity for both discipleship and community? Find an idea, an activity or an event that would help to develop either community or discipleship within the group or between groups. Staff or council members may work individually or together, looking at their own ministries or the parish at large.

Discuss any obstacles or problems with which you might have to deal, such as time, finances or personalities. Consider the group itself, the larger parish community and any concerns that surface from the outside community. Plan strategies to get through or around difficulties. Name people in the parish who might be willing to give some energy to this particular idea. If you have chosen to work individually, bring the idea back to the whole staff or council for additional input.

Final prayer and reading. Read Mark 4:3-9, repeating verse 9. Ask the group to reflect on the last verse. What helps them to hear God's voice more clearly? What are some ways that might help them to hear Christ's voice in his people? End with shared prayer or by celebrating liturgy together.

Summing Up

This exercise will help your parish staff or council come together by sharing a common vision: parish as a community of Christ's disciples. Sometimes we become so absorbed in our own particular ministries that we forget that parish staffs are also called to be a community of *disciples*. We are all learners, apprenticed to the same community. We would do well to work together, learning from each other by sharing our successes and failures. Such a demonstration of faith would be a wonderful way of modeling Christian community for the parishes we serve.

For a more comprehensive process of evaluating faith formation at your parish see my *Faith Formation: A Parish Planning Workbook,* published jointly by the National Pastoral Life Center and St. Anthony Messenger Press.

CHAPTER THREE

The Role of the Catechetical Leader

For more than thirty years I have worked in catechesis, eighteen of those years as a director of religious education. My early years as director were mostly spent organizing the formal religious education classes. That task was never easy, but textbooks, set curriculums and scope-and-sequence charts gave it some definition. Much has changed over the years. Today we find ourselves at the beginning of a new millennium with a renewed vision that emphasizes catechesis as formational as well as instructional. Our job is not nearly as clear-cut or focused. If the Church expects to flourish, however, we must accept the new challenges and reshape the way we catechize.

What's in a Name?

This shift in emphasis has taken place gradually. For me the transition began in 1984 when Dr. Tom Walters gave a talk to our archdiocesan professional organizations on his national survey profiling directors of religious education. He asked us to respond to one of the questions on the survey: "Which of the following terms most accurately describes your actual functions as director of religious education?" The eight choices were: director, administrator, catechetical leader, coordinator, pastoral minister, educator, facilitator and programmer.

I had to think about my answer a while. I knew I was a director; it was written on my office door: "Director of Religious Education." Yet, I spent much of my time coordinating and programming classes and activities for the different age groups in the parish. I also knew I was an administrator, since I drew up the budget, ordered the supplies, kept track of catechists' certification and so on. I had two degrees that told me I was an educator. Certainly I was responsible for training catechists, teaching sacramental preparation classes and leading adult education. I liked being a pastoral minister, lending a sympathetic ear and offering simple advice to the young people, parents and catechists who came to my door. And I did my best to be a facilitator, trying to make the jobs of catechists and parents a little easier. Answering that one simple question posed difficult choices!

The only response I did not even consider was that of "catechetical leader." I knew what both words meant, of course, but the title was completely foreign to me. Even though I had read the works of Thomas Groome, Maria Harris and most of the other experts in the field, in my mind, catechesis, religious education and religious instruction were all the same thing.

My response to another question on the Walters survey eventually helped me to make informed distinctions: "How effective do you feel the present classroom model (one to one and a half hours a week) of religious education is?" In our archdiocese 51 percent of the religious educators said they believed that the classroom model of religious education was either *basically or totally inadequate*. As a result of that response a task force was formed to look into alternative models of religious education. In effect, our professional organizations said: If we do not think what we are doing is working, then it is our responsibility to find some ways that do work.

Finding Alternative Models

The task force studied what theorists and practitioners in the catechetical field were saying and doing. We looked at the current culture and its impact on people's belief systems. Eventually, we connected with the New England Conference of Diocesan Directors when the Alternative Models Network was being formed. Over the next ten years we communicated with people from across the country, exchanging our thoughts and ideas on new approaches to catechesis.

We realized that for many young people and adults the spark of faith given at Baptism had never been kindled, and so we learned how indispensable evangelization was to catechesis. We learned about the essential role of the community in the formation of faith for young and old: the importance of learning by living through the liturgical, social and service activities of the parish. We learned how crucial the family is, not only in the faith formation of children but of adult members as well. And we discovered how parishes far and wide were involving adults in their own faith development. In short, we learned that we needed more than new models of religious education. We needed to renew our whole vision of catechesis, becoming more deliberate in helping youngsters and adults become active partners in the lifelong process of conversion, renewal and catechesis.

In 1997, when the *General Directory for Catechesis* was published, the catechetical world was given a tremendous resource. The *Directory* supports everything the task force had learned over the years. It offers a vision of catechesis that can renew not only local parishes but the Church itself. It reminds us that the primary aim of catechesis is to put people in intimate communion with Jesus Christ (*GDC* #80) and offers the baptismal catechumenate as an inspirational model for all catechesis:

> [T]he concept of the baptismal catechumenate *as a process of formation and as a true school of the faith* offers post-baptismal catechesis dynamic and particular characteristics: comprehensive and integrity of formation; its gradual character expressed in definite stages; its connection with meaningful rites, symbols, biblical and liturgical signs; its constant references to the Christian community. (*GDC* #91)

We know that religious instruction is only a part of catechesis. Directors of religious education need to focus on the broader concept of what catechetical leadership means in our parishes today. The functions Dr. Walters named in his 1984 survey were right on target for directors of religious education then, and by referencing the *General Directory* we see that they are applicable for parish catechetical leaders today.

Facilitator

A facilitator is someone who makes things easier, and this is the responsibility of the catechetical leader. It is the leader's job to make it easier for people to connect with God, each other and the larger Church (*GDC* #156). Catechetical leaders are evangelizers. They till the soil so the seed, the word of God, can take root and flourish (Mark 4:3-8, *GDC* #15). The catechetical leader is the one who must inspire trust and build community, listen well and accept people where they are. The catechetical leader is responsible for being open to adapting, bending and changing anything (as long as it is compatible to the gospel and in communion with the universal Church), to be inclusive of people's culture or personal needs (*GDC* #104). The catechetical leader is a facilitator.

Coordinator

The catechetical leader is responsible for coordinating catechesis within the life of the community (*GDC* #272, 273). There are two principle means of completing the tasks of catechesis: transmitting the gospel message and experiencing Christian life (*GDC* #87). The catechetical leader's job goes beyond coordinating religious education programs and touches every aspect of parish life. Catechesis is an apprenticeship: learning by doing. The Sunday liturgy as well as the parish festival are catechetical opportunities. It is the catechetical leader who must help coordinate both religious instruction and those activities that prepare for and are derived from catechesis (*GDC* #276). This means balancing liturgy with service, service with community, community with liturgy and, finally, education with liturgy, community and service.

Programmer

In light of what has been said, it follows that catechetical leaders need to be innovative programmers. They need to design and schedule a variety of activities, weaving catechesis into the fabric of parish life. Responsible catechesis means programming religious education for different age groups in peer, family and intergenerational settings and in both small groups and large groups. But it also means planning, preparing and scheduling special liturgies and prayer services, social gatherings and service opportunities for those same groups. It involves arranging for mentoring and networking, empowering others to share their faith as well as their expertise in the various ministries inside and outside the parish community. This "variety of methods is a sign of life and richness as well as a demonstration of respect for those to whom catechesis is addressed" (*GDC* #148).

Administrator

Catechetical leaders are administrators working with budgets, time management, space allotment and personnel problems. Setting up a budget for catechesis that is formational as well as instructional is a little more complicated than planning for a year of religious education classes. How money is budgeted tells a lot about one's true vision of catechesis. Money needs to be allotted for hospitality: food for fellowship, as well as comfortable furnishings and accessories that provide a welcoming environment. Money ought to be budgeted for social communication: video and audio libraries, Web sites and media literacy programs. When budgeting for textbooks, we also need to budget for home resources for adults and young people.

The catechetical leader should also be involved in the parish scheduling process, voicing how parish space and property are utilized. The leader must be able to manage people by inspiring confidence and providing support and leadership. That requires that the leader be both practical and visionary (an uncommon combination in the same person!), that is, realistic about parish resources and optimistic about parish potential.

Educator

Catechetical leaders must be well-versed in psychology and sociology, as well as current pedagogical theories and practices. But even so, helping others to grow into intimate communion with Jesus Christ requires an education beyond these secular sciences. It requires a "divine pedagogy" based on God's own methods of revelation and drawing others into relationship. Part Three of the *General Directory* instructs catechetical leaders in divine pedagogy, an inspirational model for communicating the revelations of faith (*GDC* #137).

We learn from divine pedagogy that:

- God's self-revelation happened within the everyday life of the people, peak moments of joy and sorrow as well as the everyday experiences of breaking bread. This is also where catechesis needs to be rooted in our parishes: in the life experiences of the people and in the communal celebrations of those experiences.

- God chose a people and Jesus gathered the twelve. Catechesis takes place in, with and through community. The community is the *locus* (center) of catechesis (*GDC* #158).

- God's self-revelation unfolded gradually, through the age of patriarchs, the time of the prophets, to the final revelation in the person of Jesus. Parish catechesis, too, is a gradual, life-long endeavor that nurtures, integrates and assimilates our little ones, young people and adults into the family of faith. Finally, Jesus walked with the people. Jesus was both teacher and friend. He taught in parables and plain language but mostly by example. His followers came to know him by eating, laughing, talking, walking, celebrating and serving with him. The catechetical leader is called to do the same.

Pastoral Minister

A catechetical leader is also a pastoral minister, a designation that describes an overall disposition rather than a specific function. "Pastoral minister" is not a hat that one wears, rather it is the person one becomes. The ministerial role is part of all the functions we have set out. Like Jesus, she is present to each person and situation. Like Jesus she is inclusive, a healer and reconciler. Like Jesus she teaches by her own example of love and service. And like Jesus she is both teacher and friend.

Director

A director is the person entrusted with setting the vision and direction of a corporate endeavor. For the catechetical leader, however, the vision is already set: helping people to grow toward an intimate communion with Jesus Christ. The model for accomplishing such intimacy is the baptismal cate-chumenate, a work of the whole community. The catechetical leader, as director, works with the parish to set its direction, incorporating all of the parish ministries into the catechetical framework of parish. The parish itself becomes the curriculum.[1]

The pastor is the primary director of catechesis. He is also responsible for engaging the laity to serve as catechetical leaders (GDC #224). Often this means delegating the role of director to another person, hence the DRE. The catechetical director is responsible for setting the direction and sharing the vision of catechesis with parish leadership and the parish itself. If the parish is the curriculum, the catechetical director must take the lead in setting the scope and determining the sequence.

Summing Up

This is a new enterprise for many of us, a shift in our focus. Engaging the whole parish in catechesis means an adjustment in how we spend our time and energy. No one person can fulfill all of the functions described here. Catechesis that involves the whole parish in evangelizing, forming and instructing people in the faith requires a number of catechetical leaders. The director also shares the pastor's responsibility to delegate. In faith we proclaim, "We are the body of Christ." The process of catechesis, done well, is an opportunity to live out that proclamation.

CHAPTER FOUR

Setting Up a Parish Video Library

The first weekend I took care of my nearly two-year-old grandson I noticed something unusual in his diaper bag. Tucked right between Jake's special cup and his favorite book was a videocassette. I have to admit I was a little hesitant about using the video because I did not want to make the television a baby-sitter. However, that first morning, after an hour of playing blocks and trucks, and another half hour of chasing Jake around the house as he discovered every electrical outlet that I had forgotten to buy protectors for, I was grateful to plug the video into our VCR. I discovered that cuddling up at eight in the morning with a two-year-old and watching *Barney On Broadway* could be a wonderful bonding experience.

Videotapes are here to stay. You can rent or buy them in drugstores, gas stations and supermarkets, and borrow them from public libraries. In some libraries, almost as many videos are checked out as are adult books. As individuals and families buy videos to start their own collections, so, too, parishes are following suit.

A few years ago, the parish where I worked was given a grant to start a video library. The library, it turned out, added a whole new dimension to all phases of parish life. For example, the parish purchased videos for liturgical training; videos on aging parents, divorce, communicating with teens and stress and the family proved to be excellent resources for pastoral counseling.

Instead of borrowing educational videos from the diocese,

as we used to do, we purchased them. Having the videos on hand allowed us to lend them to parishioners. Parents used the videos to work with their own children or to reinforce material originally presented by a catechist. Repeatedly, we found that adults took home videos shown in adult education sessions or in small groups; they wanted to view them or to share them with a spouse or friend. The videos most often used, however, were those classified as entertainment. As I listened to parents express appreciation to the parish for providing a source of wholesome, free entertainment, I realized what a valuable service we were offering. It took effort to get the parish video library started, but with parish backing and a good coordinating team much of the work was disbursed.

How can your parish start a video library? Consider the following steps.

Build Support for the Idea

You will need to win the support of the parish staff and the congregation. The more enthusiastic they are, the better your chance of success. Present the idea as a "total parish" endeavor, not just a religious education project. Point out the advantages to each ministry and to the parish as a whole. You might provide a list of videos relevant to each ministry or a catalog with the appropriate pages marked. Videos can be used for liturgical training and parish retreats. The video library can become a valuable resource for families or individuals looking for quality, values-oriented entertainment. Using parishioners' camcorders, you might try producing your own videos and adding them to the library. For example, consider producing a video for new parishioners to inform them about the activities, services and opportunities for service your parish offers.

To engender enthusiasm among the congregation, use direct mail, bulletin announcements, announcements at Sunday liturgies and personal contacts at parish meetings. Ask other parish ministers to mention the project at their own meetings. Let the parish know that you are beginning to develop a parish video library. Make sure they understand that it will contain not only educational, spiritual and inspirational material, but also wholesome videos for home entertainment. Ask for feedback concerning the idea. Suggest people interested in helping with the project call you.

Set Up a Coordinating Team

The team should be made up of people from various ministries, as well as parish representatives from different age groups. When our parish began setting up the library, I found it helpful to have a professional librarian join us. She proved invaluable on the practical aspects, such as what to order, where to order from and how to set up the library.

The team's first tasks are: (1) finding the money needed and (2) drawing up a survey to distribute to parishioners to find out what topics and themes are of interest. You might also ask which feature films they feel would be worth adding to the collection. The survey provides a valuable resource for future ordering and also serves as a marketing tool to promote the project.

Secure Funding

It is probably best to try a variety of approaches. Some parishes take up a special collection or sponsor a fundraiser. People are usually fairly generous when asked to contribute money for a specific project, especially if it is personally beneficial. Ask various parish groups—the men's group or the Parent Teacher Association—for donations. Suggest that the pastor or staff budget some money every year earmarked for the video library to ensure that it can be kept current in each area of ministry. Some parishes help finance their libraries by charging a nominal lending fee, fifty cents or a dollar per video. Other parishes charge a yearly family membership fee, also nominal.

To keep start-up costs low—and perhaps once or twice each year as an ongoing way of operating—ask parishioners to donate their favorite movies or children's videos. When we set up our library, we approached a large local video store, asking for help. They donated plastic video cases and storage boxes and ordered commercial videos for us, charging us only the wholesale price plus postage and handling. As an incentive, we offered them a "thank you" ad in our video library catalog.

Order the Videocassettes

Evaluate the parish survey to determine categories of interest. If you do not already have a number of catalogs on hand, call your diocesan media center, asking for a list of video suppliers. Request catalogs directly from the suppliers. Before you order, consult with the diocesan media expert to learn which videos are best for each subject category and age group you are interested in. Many videos can be used to great effect by the whole family or whole parish, even though they may be listed as "children's videos." Because videos are expensive and you are ordering for the long term, you may want to preview videos before you order them. Try checking out any that interest you from the diocesan media center.

Gather various groups to preview videos targeted to their age or interest. Show short excerpts from a number of different videos and ask for evaluations. Be sure to observe the reactions of these previewers as they watch the videos.

Ask the team members to help determine selections. If you have asked a mother of preschoolers to be part of the team, for example, you might ask her to host and facilitate one preview, inviting the parents and children of that age group. She can observe and facilitate the evaluation process and report to the team. Also, make sure you check with leaders of each of the parish ministries for ideas. Suggest they order their own videos for previewing, and make them responsible for preview gatherings and evaluations.

Before buying even the best of videos, ask yourself, "How often do I think this video will be used?" If you think it will be used rarely, consider borrowing it from the diocesan media center as needed, rather than purchasing it.

Promote the Cause

One of the best ways to promote the library is by involving as many people as you can in planning and previewing. Youngsters and oldsters will likely see in the sampling at least one video to catch their interest. They will want to see more, anticipating the library's grand opening, when they can find the video they recommended and check it out. Regularly make use of the parish's weekly bulletin. Describe the latest purchase and list seasonal materials. Occasionally you might have enough material to merit a bulletin insert.

Our parish hung a bulletin board across the hall from the video library, highlighting various video offerings. We also published a catalog describing the videos, with cross-references to help determine appropriate age group and subject matter. Library hours, procedures and penalties for overdue videos were noted in the catalog. Our best marketing venture was an occasional open house held on a Friday night or Sunday afternoon. We borrowed several televisions and video recorders to set up in different rooms at the parish, and ran a selection of movies, cartoons, educational and inspirational videos for about three hours. We provided two or three small video players for individuals to preview the video of their choice. We served popcorn, chips, hot dogs and soda pop. A week in advance, we always published the open-house times and the videos to be shown. In that way people could arrive whenever they wanted. Families could either stay together or go their separate ways.

Maintain the Library

You need to decide where your library will be, when it will be open and what rules you would like to set down for operating it. You also need to find people to staff the library. Place was no problem for our parish: We built a lockable wooden cabinet into our already existing parish library. Another parish I know about solved a space shortage problem by storing its videos on library carts they wheeled out after each Sunday Mass. Sometimes they tied balloons to the carts so people could find them easily. The point is to make sure the videos are accessible. Keeping videos in a school building next to the church may limit their use.

Establish and post simple rules and procedures for the video library. How long is the check-out period? How many videos can a family or an individual take at one time? What is the penalty for an overdue video? How does one sign up or enroll to use the library?

Summing Up

If it is true that the television set is the gathering place for this generation as the fireplace was for generations past, the parish has an opportunity to help people use that time to its best advantage. Watching television together has advantages. Like a good storyteller or an engaging play, a video can offer people an opportunity to experience (and sometimes to discuss) a common activity together. After my weekend experience with grandson Jake, I can understand why parents (and even some grandmas) are creating video libraries alongside their books. If a parish can afford it—and perhaps even more in parishes where individual families may not be able to afford their own video collections—it may be time for parishes to invest in a video library. It is another way to serve the whole community by offering material worth viewing.

CHAPTER FIVE

Visions and Tasks for the Future

I spent Pentecost weekend several years ago at a seminar envisioning catechesis for the twenty-first century. Here I discovered the proverb cited in the Preface to this book: "A vision without a task is a dream. A task without a vision is drudgery. A vision and a task is the hope of the world." Setting some visions and discussing the corresponding tasks were the weekend's objectives.

People from religious education offices and parishes in forty-seven different dioceses attended the roundtable seminar, sponsored by the Catechetical Renewal Network. By design, one-fourth of the participants were a mix of young adults—parish and campus youth ministers, university students and singles and young parents from local parishes. Their presence grounded us in the reality of today's world, and reminded us of the challenges and possibilities of tomorrow's.

Four major presentations on Friday night and Saturday reflected the ideas put forward in the *General Directory for Catechesis*. The presenters were all pillars in the catechetical community: Father Robert Hater started the seminar, leading a discussion on evangelization. Françoise Darcy-Berube talked about initiatory catechesis as an inspirational model. Dr. Tom Walters spoke on Catholic literacy and Dick Reichert presented adult catechesis as a parish priority.

For each topic the process was the same: An opening prayer and Scripture followed a speaker's presentation. After five minutes of silence, a young adult offered a second, briefer reflection on the same topic. Another five minutes of silence preceded thirty to forty minutes of table discussion. Finally, each group was asked to come up with a banner statement followed by a few brief sentences summarizing their discussion.

On Pentecost Sunday, participants assimilated what they had heard and experienced by reading the journals they had been given for keeping notes from the presentations and the table summaries. After longer periods for silent prayer the tables reassembled. Each table group was asked to articulate a vision for future catechesis, and then to prepare a strategy, naming some of the tasks necessary to make the vision a reality in their parishes or dioceses.

I now share with you the visions and tasks of the various tables, combined and synthesized into five banner statements. What you read here are my own interpretations of their brief summary statements. (All quotes without citations from the *General Directory* are taken from the table summaries.)

Community as the Curriculum

The vision: "We share our story, we break our bread, and we proclaim our rising from the dead." We are called to proclaim this new life in Christ not only at Sunday liturgy but through all our communal statements and actions. The everyday life of a parish—its ministries, its rituals—forms and sustains its members. Everything about parish life teaches us what it means to be a Catholic. Catechesis is about apprenticeship, about learning while doing, and it is a lifelong endeavor.

The Rite of Christian Initiation of Adults recognizes the gradual, incremental nature of the process. It takes time for fellowship to develop among people, for building relationships and community. The process connects the person with meaningful rites, symbols and biblical and liturgical signs. This is why the *General Directory for Catechesis* tells us that the baptismal catechumenate (the initiatory process) is the model for all catechesis (*GDC* #90). It presumes the Christian community's role as primary catechist.

The tasks: As Françoise Darcy-Berube pointed out, such a pastoral approach requires cooperation and integration, creativity and flexibility. Hospitality is crucial. Everything, from the message on our answering machines to the furniture in our meeting rooms, is important. Everyone, from the parish secretary to the pastor, needs to be welcoming. We must be deliberate in designing opportunities for people to meet and get to know each other. We must be creative in developing new rituals and rites to mark important occasions and events in people's lives. Since the Church is truly the Body of Christ, what better teacher can there be? "Catechetical pedagogy will be effective to the extent that the Christian community becomes a point of concrete reference for the faith journey of individuals. This happens when the community is proposed as a source, *locus* and means of catechesis" (*GDC* #158).

Integrating Initiation and Schooling

The vision: "Discipleship comes through integrating initiation and schooling and leads to service." Tom Walters did an excellent job of distinguishing between the processes of initiation and schooling. Christians who have been initiated in the basic elements of faith need continuing and ongoing education in that faith. This education is called "continuing catechesis" or "permanent catechesis" (*GDC* #51).

The tasks: Faith seeks knowledge. If the faith we experience is to be assimilated, it needs definition, words and stories that can help shape it and provide meaning and structure. While this may take place during the process of initiation, it needs to be highlighted by formal or informal instruction. Since the process of initiation and education both have limitations, it is to our advantage to set realistic desired outcomes for each.

We also need flexibility about what we expect to accomplish: literacy levels, for example, based on the different groups gathered (youth, children, catechists, adults, catechumens). If we hope to communicate our faith to each other and hand it on to the next generation, we need words and stories that express our experience of faith. The questions are How many words? and Which stories? "It is fundamentally important that catechesis for adults, whether baptized or not, initiatory catechesis for children and young people and continuing catechesis are closely linked with the catechetical endeavor of the Christian community, so that the particular Church may grow harmoniously and that its evangelizing activity may spring from authentic sources" (*GDC* #72).

Intergenerational Communities

The vision: "Our vision is of a community of disciples of all ages and backgrounds who are enthusiastic about building the kingdom." While there are certainly specific times when people, young and old, need the company and support of their peers, Church by its nature is intergenerational. All ages worship together at Sunday liturgy.

The tasks: Why not offer opportunities for various age groups to learn and serve side by side? It seems obvious that the more Christian adults accompany a young person on his or her faith journey, the richer that young person's experience will be. Adults involved in intergenerational groups also know that such arrangements are reciprocal; children and teenagers have much to offer adults.

Perhaps if the Church became more deliberate in modeling life-giving intergenerational learning, the "domestic church" (that is, the family) might follow suit. It is important to remember that intergenerational learning begins in the home. How can we ensure that family catechesis is a parish priority? By encouraging parents to talk about their faith, read stories from Scripture and pray with their children. Parishes can provide home resources as well as opportunities for families to meet with other families for support and encouragement. We need "to create an environment that will facilitate and empower families to focus themselves on Jesus and live the gospel message." It is to everyone's advantage to encourage families and parish intergenerational groupings by planning special times to pray, play, work, learn and serve together for children, teens, adults and the aged. "Thus a fundamental dialogue between the generations can be promoted both within the family and within the community" (*GDC* #188).

A Holistic Approach to Catechesis

The vision: "Catechesis is life itself." It is not a separate compartment *in* our lives. It cannot be relegated to a particular place or specific time. Individuals discover God and learn about God in their own ways, in their own time, and through their own filters and lenses. We need to "listen to the pulse of the Spirit in the people of God in their cultural environment." Remember, culture is not limited to one's ethnic group. The young and the old, the person from rural, urban and suburban settings all have their own "cultures."

The tasks: As catechists, we must engage people where we find them, to learn their language and use it. To engage young people, for example, we need not only to become comfortable with technology but also, as some participants suggested, *to sacramentalize it*. We do not bring God into people's lives; God is already there. Our job is to help people make connections.

Parishes need a variety of approaches, acknowledging that different people need different things at different times. We must create both quiet spaces and communal situations: listening opportunities to tap into what lies at the heart of all people—universal questions of life, death and suffering. (For more about this, see Robert H. Hater's *The Search for Meaning*, Crossroads, 1998.) One of the concrete tasks of catechesis is "making the Catechumenate and catechetical institutes into 'centers of inculturation,' incorporating, with discernment, the language, symbols, and values of the cultures in which the catechumens and those to be catechized live" (*GDC* #110).

A Community of Disciples

The vision: "We are a community that experiences the liberating and unconditional love of God individually and in common, responding to our baptismal call to discipleship through prayer, Scripture and witness." All of the presenters at the Pentecost weekend seminar spoke of the need to focus on one of the primary reasons for Church: to proclaim the good news and help bring about the reign of God. Dick Reichert especially challenged us to look at what it means to be a disciple.

The tasks: As catechists we have done a fairly good job of helping people realize that God loves them. Our responsibility to proclaim the Good News, however, demands more. We must also help people to realize that their response to God's love always involves working to bring about God's reign. All Christians are called to work for peace and justice, to love not just our friends but our enemies, to give not just from our bounty but from our sustenance.

What is discipleship, and how do we form and foster it? "Discipleship is messy...but it is to do what Jesus would do: reach out to others, share their stories, empower people to serve by recognizing their gifts and encouraging them." True catechists live their lives as committed disciples. When we become a community of such disciples, the Church will be what it was always meant to be. This is the Church we are called to build, and if we build it, they will come. "...Catechesis shall arouse in catechumens and those receiving catechesis 'a preferential option for the poor'...which 'far from being a sign of individualism and sectarianism, makes manifest the universality of the Church's nature and mission. This option is not exclusive'...but implies 'a commitment to justice, according to each individual's role, vocation and circumstance'..." (*GDC* #104).

Summing Up

I left that Pentecost weekend filled with energy and enthusiasm. Unfortunately, it did not take long for reality to set in again. Immediate needs and the demands for my time began to drain all my newfound energy. It is so much easier to dream and envision and believe that all things are possible when you are surrounded by enthusiastic, faith-filled people! I keep thinking of what could be accomplished if that Pentecost experience were a regular happening. What if people, young and old, came together on a regular basis to listen and learn, to pray together and share their experiences along with their hopes and dreams?

But that, of course, is and always has been "the vision"—a Pentecost experience every Sunday—a eucharistic celebration in which one is surrounded by enthusiastic, faith-filled people, the body of Christ broken and shared, who support and encourage each other as they leave the assembly and live the message at home and in their workplace. It is our task as catechetical leaders to find ways for this to happen. This is our vision, on to the tasks.

Part Two
Message, Community, Service

Introduction

While these three essential elements [message, community and service] can be separated for the sake of analysis, they are joined in the one educational ministry. Each educational program or institution under Church sponsorship is obliged to contribute in some way to the realization of the threefold purpose within the total educational ministry.
—To Teach as Jesus Did, #14

I started working on my master's degree in theology in the mid-seventies when the bishops' pastoral *To Teach as Jesus Did* *(TTJD)* was stimulating a lot of discussion. During that time my husband and I also volunteered as coordinators of the parish youth program. I learned much about the document from the catechetical course I took; I learned more from working with young people in our youth group.

The pastoral talks about the three interlocking dimensions of catechesis: message, service and community. My work in youth ministry validated this integrated approach, but experience taught me that each element is both the end and a means of catechesis. The three dimensions overlap and conjoin, but working with teens taught me to begin with community and service. We were always delivering the message, but it was more readily internalized after young people had spent time working together in service and bonding in Christian community. It is in that order that the elements are presented: community, service and message.

Twenty years of working in family catechesis also taught

me that all three interlocking elements are fundamental to the Christian family. And so this section of *Practical Catechesis* begins with the chapter, *"To Teach as Jesus Did,"* and ends with an account of my experience in Russia, where I witnessed the fruit of all three catechetical components.

CHAPTER SIX

To Teach as Jesus Did:
Family Catechesis

In their 1972 pastoral letter *To Teach as Jesus Did*, the U.S. Catholic bishops presented a new vision of Catholic education. They described it as an integrated ministry embracing three important interlocking dimensions: (1) message (*didache*)—"the message revealed by God which the Church proclaims"; (2) community (*koinonia*)—"fellowship in the life of the Holy Spirit"; and (3) service (*diakonia*)—"to the Christian community and the entire human community."

This threefold way of looking at catechesis reminds us that doctrine is not merely a matter of the intellect, that community lived is community learned, and that service is an effective way to discover one's faith. Successful catechesis, then, is not measured by how well Catholics know the catechism, but how well they hear the gospel message of hope, respond to it in love and service and grow closer to Christ in life-giving, personal relationships. All three interlocking dimensions are best learned and lived in the everyday experience of family.

Whether or not they realized it at the time, the bishops had offered a vision of Catholic education that looks beyond the confines of the classroom. In the ensuing years their vision was enthusiastically taken up by religious educators who struggled to adapt existing programs and institutions in light of it. But pouring the "new wine" into the old "wineskins" of religious education was anything but easy.

While it was difficult to move beyond the classroom model, long considered synonymous with Catholic education, it did not take long to discover that simply calling a classroom a Christian community does not make it one. Nor does collecting cans of vegetables for the food pantry automatically qualify as a faith experience. The move from catechesis that is classroom-centered to catechesis rooted in community and discovered in service is more like a "paradigm shift."

A paradigm shift is a little like an earthquake: foundations seem to tremble. For educators, such movement can seem perilously unresponsive to direction. What can Catholics do while the ground is shaking? We catechetical leaders have begun to look more closely at the whole process of catechesis, redefining objectives and clarifying language. We understand that the purpose of catechesis is to enliven, activate and make conscious one's faith, as well as to impart theological knowledge (*Sharing the Light of Faith*, National Catechetical Directory for Catholics of the United States, #32). The question is: How does the parish today best fulfill its catechetical role?

The Struggle to Adapt

Not long ago, belonging to a church or a synagogue and professing a belief in God was considered to be part of the "American way." The extended family and neighborhood supported parents as they passed on their own faith to their children. Even the entertainment industry supported basic Judeo-Christian values. Everybody, it seemed, professed some faith, whether they were Catholic or Lutheran, Baptist or Jewish. For Catholics, faith was a part of one's identity.

With this supportive base in family and culture, religious educators were able to concentrate their lessons on what it means to be a Catholic. Classroom learning served as an effective model of religious education for more than a century and may have been adequate when one's faith and religious heritage were an integral part of one's life. It is not adequate today. American culture and American Catholics have changed. We cannot presume that adults and young people attending parish religious education programs today have experienced either the faith or the heritage into which they were baptized.

Catechesis is a formational process that ought to begin early in life and continue throughout it. While evangelization in its broadest sense encompasses catechesis, catechesis is an essential "moment" in the process of evangelization (*GDC* #63), and also involves the formational process of pre-evangelization, evangelization and, finally, a more formal, instructional catechesis. This process is sequence and overlap.

Pre-evangelization is a time for building relationships and creating a safe and welcoming environment. Evangelization is proclaiming (not explaining) the gospel as well as bearing witness to one's personal faith. We recognize the importance of both as essential elements in the process of the Rite of Christian Initiation of Adults.

Pre-evangelization and evangelization can happen anywhere. They used to happen for children on neighborhood swing sets and in grandma's kitchen. That is seldom the case today. The world has changed dramatically in the last thirty years. Adults as well as children have lost a basic sense of security. Safe, welcoming environments and meaningful relationships are often hard to come by. If we want our children to grow up embracing the Catholic faith, parents and parishes will need to look beyond the classroom model. If we want parents and other adults to grow in their faith, parish catechetical leaders will need to be more deliberate in their catechetical planning. Family catechesis is one way to meet the needs of both children and adults.

In family catechesis we offer parents the tools and resources they need to explore their own faith and share that faith with their young people. (The parish's role in evangelizing young people is the topic of a later chapter.) By helping families grow in their commitment to the faith, parishes reaffirm the family as the center of Christian experience. They realize that the Christian family, by its nature, affirms and nurtures community and service to each other within the everyday give and take of family life. Table blessings, night prayers and faith stories shared from Scripture and personal experience all convey the Christian message. Promoting and supporting family catechesis within the parish is to everyone's advantage. The process can take place at the parish as well as in homes.

Parish-Based Programs

These programs almost always have an intergenerational component; however, they are not limited to households or family units. The *whole* parish is invited. The sessions usually include process-oriented activities: crafts, music and games, as well as religious instruction. Participants are asked to take part in both large-group and small-group intergenerational activities. In most cases families come together once or twice a month and meet for approximately two hours. Material is sent home to continue the learning process.

Some parishes facilitate parish-based family programs that separate into peer groups for the instructional component. Adults and youngsters meet at the parish at the same time, preferably twice a month. At the beginning of the session, all age groups gather together to set the theme with a prayer or Scripture reading, sometimes followed by an icebreaker or some other activity. Then age groups meet separately. Adults are divided into smaller groups, either according to interests (single parents, young adults and so on) or heterogeneously. It is important that people remain in the same groups for each meeting in order to develop trust and establish relationships. At the end of the session, all participants reassemble for the closing. It may be a simple prayer or an activity or game in which participants summarize the day's theme, staying in the intergenerational groups. The closing exercise is usually followed by a social time. Parents/guardians are given additional material to share with their youngsters at home.

Home-Based Family Catechesis

Family catechesis is different from home-schooling since adults as well as children are the targeted learners, and sometimes three or more family groups work together. In addition, educators speak of "gathering households," which means extending the invitation beyond the nuclear family.

One example of family home-based catechesis comes from Peru. A representative parent from each neighborhood meets once a week with the parish director of religious education. At that meeting, the DRE prepares the parents to teach a specific lesson. These adults return to their homes (1) to share with the other parents in the neighborhood what they have learned, and (2) to work with their own children. While this model may appear to be child-centered, its primary purpose is adult catechesis. Such neighborhood meetings are often the way small base communities are formed.

The DRE also meets once a week with a teenager from each neighborhood. The teenagers are given ideas for crafts, games or music that follow the week's lesson. The teenager returns to the neighborhood and meets with all the youngsters, usually on a Saturday morning. At the end of the unit, all parents, teenagers and children come to church for a closing celebration and party.

Catechetical Renewal

In *Catechesi Tradendae*, Pope John Paul II tells us, "Catechesis needs to be continually renewed by a certain broadening of its concepts, by the revision of its methods, by searching for suitable language, and by the utilization of new means of transmitting the message" (*CT* #17). This idea of catechetical renewal moves us beyond classrooms or specific programs and models and acknowledges that together, as members of the one body of Christ, we are called to teach as Jesus did: by what we say, by who we are and by what we do. The formational process of catechesis cannot be contained solely in programs (even the best programs) and institutions. Success will come when community, service and message finally become integrated in one ministry, a ministry active in the home, throughout the parish and in the marketplace. The threefold theme of message, community and service found in *To Teach As Jesus Did* offers us a vision of catechesis as it should be.

CHAPTER SEVEN

The Community as Catechist

A ccording to Gallup surveys, four of ten Americans have frequent or occasional feelings of intense loneliness, making us the loneliest people in the world. The Gallup Organization says that because of this fact, one of the things Americans most want from their churches is a sense of community. It is a reasonable request, and parish catechetical leaders must take this need seriously when working with both adults and children.

Community

Church is, by definition, a community. We worship together, work together and learn together. But it is not simply in togetherness that loneliness can be eased. Kneeling in a crowded church or sitting in a classroom full of second-grade parents does not satisfy the basic need to belong. We must never forget that one of the elementary tasks of being church is to offer support and fellowship to all members and hospitality to the stranger.

Sometimes we can get so wrapped up in the business of running church or the busyness of running programs that we forget about that primary task. Welcoming people and helping them to get to know each other is the job of the whole parish. Most parish renewal programs that have been around for the last few years are successful because that is precisely where they begin.

Renewal programs, such as "FOLLOW ME! Discipleship for the 21st Century," "Christ Renews His Parish" and RENEW, bring small groups of people together and offer a process that enables them to get to know each other on a personal basis and then to share their faith. Another renewal program, "Called to Be Church," is designed to restructure the entire parish into small faith communities. Churches that have experienced such renewal programs report that the community formed within the small groups carries over into the larger parish.

In most parishes, the renewal programs are designed to be facilitated by a core team of parishioners and staff. They are not usually the responsibility of the catechetical leader. Religious education goes on as usual, often with the renewal program as the hub, but not the sole resource for faith development and community building. In addition to keeping these formal programs in mind, we also need to be mindful of finding other ways to build and support community—practical methods that are helpful even if a parish is not involved in a formal renewal program.

Building Community With Adults

In an informal way, you can promote community by helping parishioners get to know each other whenever they are gathered. Providing name tags and asking some people to serve as greeters at parent meetings is a good start. This type of simple hospitality helps people feel welcomed and comfortable as they put names to the faces they see on Sunday mornings. A table with coffee, cider and doughnuts (if the parish can afford it), works much like the town well did years ago. It attracts people for simple refreshment and gives them the opportunity to share pleasantries. Once people are seated, encourage the adults to introduce themselves to the people around them.

Begin the program with some questions. For example, at a parents' Confirmation preparation meeting you might ask, What were you like when you were fourteen? or, What do you remember about your own Confirmation and the preparation that went into it? Allow enough time for people to think about their answers. You may even want to ask them to write their responses. Then, ask them to find someone that they do not know, introduce themselves and share their answers.

Try asking the following questions at a parent meeting at the beginning of the school year: If your child could only learn one thing about faith this year, what would you want it to be? Why is that important to you? After parents have thought about it and shared their response, ask them, How can you teach that one thing at home? Involving your listeners by touching on their own experiences and expectations is good catechetical process. Giving them the opportunity to share with someone else not only strengthens that process but also helps to build community.

You can help to build and support community within every group with which you interact. Education commissions, catechists and youth boards can all become small communities if you bring them together occasionally for table fellowship, retreat days or similar opportunities that allow for interaction in a non-task-oriented environment. A parish is actually a community made up of many smaller communities. By impacting those small groups that are a part of your ministry, the whole parish will reap the benefits.

Building Community With Children

Young people also need to feel they belong. They need to belong to a community of their peers; they also need to feel they are a welcomed part of the larger parish community. Once again this is the job of the entire parish; however, there are particular ways of promoting community within the catechetical program itself.

Developing a community of peers can happen rather easily in a parochial school setting. Children who meet daily have ample opportunity to form bonds. It is much more difficult when children come together only weekly for a relatively short period of time, especially when the majority of that time is spent covering material in a textbook. Unless children—especially older children—are given the opportunity to get to know each other and develop a level of trust, most classroom discussions can remain only on a superficial level.

Suggest to your catechists that at the beginning of the year, even before books are passed out, they spend a whole class period or two getting to know each other. A variety of resources and materials are available to help facilitate community building on all age levels. During this time, it is also important for the catechist to share who she is with her students. By telling children stories about herself when she was their age, her hopes and fears, the catechist will help them to feel more comfortable in talking about themselves.

Each week find out what is happening in the lives of the students and encourage them to share their concerns of the day. Provide opportunities to work with partners. Allow time occasionally for informal play. Catechists who have tried these approaches say that they make discussions throughout the year more meaningful. They also say that because they know each child's situation, they can personalize lessons and highlight issues pertinent to each group.

Youngsters learn the meaning of church, not from some textbook, but by observing the parish around them. The only way they will understand what Christian community means is by feeling that they are a part of the witnessing community themselves. Sometimes a parish needs to ask itself what it does, outside of providing a parochial school or religious education program, that makes its children feel they are respected members.

Do we respect their need to worship as children by providing a children's Liturgy of the Word at Sunday Masses? Do we have special scheduled events just for them, which bring them to church to interact with their peers and adults in a social setting? Children are not just the Church of tomorrow; they are the Church today. As such they deserve to have all their ministerial needs met. (For more ideas see "Evangelizing and Catechizing Our Children" in Part Four.) Finally, do the children in our religious education programs feel comfortable in our parochial school classrooms?

Religious Education and Catholic Schools

I have heard DREs ask this last question more often than any other: How can we make sure that children who don't attend the parochial school do not feel like second-rate parishioners? Too often these children are told not to touch or to move anything in the classroom. They cannot use the chalkboards or display their work. They are made acutely aware of the fact that they are sitting in someone else's desk, in someone else's classroom. It must be difficult for children to feel that they are a part of church, that they belong, when their only experience of church is at an adult service on Sunday and an hour or so each week in a borrowed classroom.

In many parishes, DREs and principals are working together to alleviate this problem. They are helping catechists and teachers come together to find ways of sharing classroom space and materials. Religious education students are given bulletin board space. Children who share the same desk exchange written messages and are occasionally brought together. These parishes have come to realize that Catholic education and Catholic schools are not and should not be synonymous. All parish children deserve a first-rate program and are entitled to parish space.

Summing Up

People, young and old, need to feel they belong, that they are part of a community. That is what it means to be church. We are a community of Christ's disciples. It is often in that basic longing to be with others that the initial call to discipleship is heard. When the need to be welcomed, accepted and supported is met in Christian fellowship, the spirit of that community is free to share itself as Body of Christ with the world. Individually and collectively that spirit can become active in everyday lives, but it all begins with community. "Where two or three are gathered in my name, I am there among them" (Matthew 18:20).

CHAPTER EIGHT

The Catechesis of Christian Service

S everal years ago, a young neighbor stopped by to ask if he could baby-sit for me. He said he would work at no cost, but that it had to be that evening. I thanked him politely, but told him I had nowhere to go and really needed to stay home. He told me he would be willing to sit the next weekend, also for free, but the catch was this: I had to sign his Confirmation service contract that night because he needed four more hours of service if he was to be confirmed. The contract was due the next day.

The principle of requiring service hours for Confirmation seems sound enough. The ministry of service is an essential aspect of the Church's mission and is therefore an important part not only of Confirmation preparation but all catechesis. Yet if all we are teaching our young people is how to be creative in meeting a deadline, we are misusing this ministry. For service to be a legitimate part of a catechetical program, it must be more than an end in itself. Service is an effective part of catechesis for both adults and young people only when we allow the ministry itself to teach. And like so many lessons it is best learned in, with and through community.

In *To Teach as Jesus Did*, service, along with message and community, is one of the three interlocking dimensions of the educational mission of the Church. The reason these three elements are so essential to the bishops' vision for Catholic education can be found in the pastoral's title. If we observe how Jesus taught, we see that service is not just an action but a life-altering attitude fostered best in community with others.

An Attitude of Service

"What I just did was to give you an example," Jesus told the disciples after washing their feet, "as I have done so you must do" (see John 13:11-17). Jesus showed us in this and a lifetime of other actions the appropriate disposition of Christian service. When Jesus gave, he gave of himself, never posturing in superiority. He respected each individual and was totally present to those with whom he ministered. His ministry was always conjunctive.

Our Christian service must be oriented in the same way. Being of service ought to unite us to those with whom we work. It is easy to fall into the trap of becoming the benevolent giver, representing the "haves" while others are the "have nots." Yet Jesus exemplified service that is never patronizing. For the Christian, the axiom "There, but for the grace of God, go I" would better read: "There go I."

Of course, it takes more than assigning service hours to foster a genuine desire to be of service to others. Especially for young people, service must first be demonstrated before it can be nurtured. It was by walking and eating and living in community with Jesus that the disciples learned to serve. When the time came for them to go out and minister, Jesus sent them two by two (see Mark 6:7). Service can be a powerful teacher when it is practiced in community with others. Service projects taken up by small groups offer a chance to observe the examples (both negative and positive) of others and to reflect on the "shared experience."

Creating Opportunities for Service

Many parishes require candidates for Confirmation to participate in service projects with other students under adult supervision. Some have successfully involved young adults, specifically, to act as adult guides. By offering a variety of projects (cleaning elderly parishioners' yards, working in a soup kitchen or helping with summer Bible School) the candidate is given some choice about where to serve. A dozen youngsters can host a parish reception or organize an Advent party for preschool parishioners. Fundraisers, such as car washes or a parish breakfast, offer candidates the additional satisfaction of deciding upon a charity to which they will give the money they raised. It is important to spend time afterward reflecting upon the experience, discussing how the young people felt and what they learned.

Adults not only supervise the youngsters but facilitate the discussion. They may also elect to come together with other adult sponsors to talk about their own experiences of working with the young people. The most important role of the adults, however, is to exemplify in their own lives true Christian service. Just as Jesus gave his disciples an example, so the adult community must show—not just tell—young people what a life of service means. The parish outreach and the manner in which parishioners serve each other offer powerful lessons to the younger generation. When they have the additional opportunity of working on service projects side by side with adults and peers, the experience moves from the realm of "lessons about" to that of "participating in" Christian ministry.

Parish service opportunities should certainly not be limited to Confirmation preparation. Appropriate projects can be initiated on all age levels. Primary students can talk about their own experiences of being sick or shut-in, while they make tray favors for a local hospital.

Sharing the Bounty

One of my favorite service projects takes place each fall. It involves the whole parish, but especially the young people, who learn the importance of sharing with others what they have received. The children are encouraged to share their Halloween candy with young adult parishioners who are away at college or in the armed services. A week or two before Beggar's Night, parishioners receive by mail a flyer announcing the event. Parents of young adults who are away from home are asked to write their children's names and addresses on the outside of an envelope. Inside, they are asked to put a few dollars to cover the postage and wrapping. Adult parishioners are asked to donate candy left over from Beggar's Night and to volunteer to help sort and package the candy. Everyone is invited to donate candy or write notes.

The parish children also receive a flyer asking them to share their Halloween treats, not just leftovers but some of the good stuff (particularly their chocolate bars; college kids love chocolate). An evening is scheduled to bring youngsters, teenagers and adults together to sort, package and write.

The evening can be organized to include a wide range of age groups. Little children can draw pictures or write notes to be included in the packages. Some of the older children and adults can sort the candy into piles: bubble gum, lollipops, Snickers bars, etc. When everything is sorted, boxes are filled assembly-line style. Hand-written notes and pictures are included, as well as a note telling each young person that they are in the thoughts and prayers of the parish community. The evening ends with a prayer service remembering the young adults who are receiving the packages in prayer by name.

I have worked with this program in both a large suburban parish and in smaller urban churches. The response from parishioners—children and adult volunteers as well as the young people who receive the packages—has always been extremely positive. Thank-you notes come from parish young adults all over the world, an eloquent testimony to how simple it is to help young adults feel they are still part of the home parish. The program is not only a great way to evangelize such young adults but it teaches youngsters how good it feels to share, not from their parents' cupboard but from their own abundance.

City and Country Neighbors

A neighboring parish has linked with an Appalachian mission church. The two are only a few hours apart and the connection began simply enough. A parishioner in the city parish began to collect clothes for a friend in the rural church. Not long after, it became a regular event for volunteers from the Confirmation class—along with their teachers and other adults—to travel south with food, games and prizes to put on a carnival for the children in the rural parish. When the city youngsters reached high school, they found other reasons to make the trip to the mountains: Roofs needed to be mended; children needed to be tutored.

In appreciation, the women of the rural church made a beautiful quilt for the city church, depicting the Stations of the Cross. It now hangs in a place of honor in the urban church. Last summer a group of city women made the trip to Kentucky, this time to learn from their country sisters the art of quilting. Both churches are enjoying the experience of getting to know each other through mutual giving and receiving. And without anyone's intending it, the young people of both parishes are observing and practicing Christian service.

CHAPTER NINE

Catholic Literacy:
Getting the Message

I first became concerned about Catholic literacy on the night our youngest son was to receive first Penance. The family was sitting around the dinner table when I remarked about how exciting it was that Peter was about to receive a sacrament. Peter, sitting at my left, turned to me and asked, "What's a sacrament?"

I was stunned. I had been the director of religious education at our home parish for six years. I had made sure Peter had the best catechists. We were using an approved textbook series. I knew the sacraments had been a part of the scope and sequence, yet somehow my son had reached the fourth grade without learning the word *sacrament*. As I quizzed him on what was about to happen that evening, I realized that he understood the concept of "sacrament," he just did not have the word to name it.

Being an old English teacher I know the importance of vocabulary. Being an even older catechist, I know that words are essential in discussing, explaining and communicating the faith one to another, generation to generation. I also know, however, that while words are important, the choice of words and the way they are taught is even more important.

A product of the *Baltimore Catechism*, I can still recite (as can so many of my generation) a few of the definitions I learned in grade school. I also know that I have forgotten a hundred "answers" for every one that I vaguely remember. I do not want to return to those days. I do not want the precious time my grandchildren spend learning about their faith to be simply rote memorization and head learning. But the old pendulum keeps swinging, and I fear our concern about an "illiterate faithful" may try to take us back, wishfully, to a time to which we can no longer return.

Please note: I am writing as an educator, looking at a few explicit things we ought to teach our children. I am also aware that learning takes place in a much greater context of socialization. These social encounters often teach our children implicitly more than can be taught in a lesson plan.

So here is the dilemma: How can we make sure our children learn the language of faith, while we still emphasize that they experience and internalize that faith?

We can begin by being realistic in assessing how much children can memorize and retain without losing interest and attention. In other words, we need to be selective in our choice of vocabulary. And we need to be open to the many approaches to comprehending it. We also need to remember that Catholic literacy is not only about words. Catholic literacy also means knowing the stories of our faith: the inspired narratives of Scripture as well as the stories of the community.

Learning the Story of Our Faith

For a long time I have been concerned that our children, as well as many of our adults, are hearing the story of God piecemeal. Excerpts from Scripture are heard at Mass. Children's textbooks present disconnected episodes of Jesus' life. Stories of our Church are often relegated to whatever time is left over. Yet it is these stories from Holy Scripture, Church history and the lives of saints that have helped to form and define us as a people.

One of the primary reasons I decided to put together the family catechetical series, God Is Calling (St. Anthony Messenger Press), was so there could be a story-based family catechetical series that covered salvation history from the story of creation to modern-day saints. At some point young people need to hear the stories told sequentially to help them see the plan of God unfold and to see their place within it. Stories are a natural way to learn about who we are and why we are.

Some parishes, realizing the value of stories, make sure that each family not only has an adult Bible but also a children's Bible. Other parishes make a point of having their seventh or eighth graders read—as a group—one of the Gospels. To ensure that the reading holds the young people's interest, they recruit a professional storyteller or children's librarian to narrate, with or without the young people reading along. Lent is a good time to introduce this activity if you allow enough time to talk about Jesus' life, death and resurrection. The stories of our faith not only convey the essence of what we believe but also introduce the reader/listener to the vocabulary that communicates our faith.

A Basic Vocabulary

If we limit the number of words and phrases we expect our children to learn, we have a better chance of seeing that they walk away from our programs with a basic vocabulary of faith. A short list also makes it possible to introduce and reinforce the concepts over and over, year after year, in a variety of age-appropriate ways.

How short a list? Twelve words or phrases sounds like a reasonable number, an average of one or two words a month. Focusing on more dilutes concentration. Remember, the idea is to present and define these words at every grade level. This does not mean that first graders need to memorize definitions, but they can still be introduced to the words.

In this respect teaching about religion is like teaching children about their body. By using the proper terminology at an early age, you provide a good foundation for later learning. Certainly children will learn many more words and phrases than twelve, as well as names of people and places, but by naming twelve we emphasize their particular importance. A dozen words and phrases along with the basic stories of salvation history mastered by grade six sounds to me like a realistic goal for children and parish catechetical leaders.

What's on the Short List?

How do we determine the short list? The *General Directory for Catechesis* names three things as basic and essential in initiatory catechesis (and certainly the catechesis in which our youngsters are engaged, at least, pre-Confirmation, can still be considered initiatory). Initiatory catechesis is "[first] centered on what constitutes *the nucleus of Christian experience,* [second] the *most fundamental certainties of faith,* and [third] the *most essential evangelical values*" (*GDC* #67. Emphasis added.). So who determines that second element? What are the most fundamental certainties of faith our children need to learn?

Personally, rather than considering putting together their own textbook series, I would like to see our bishops come up with a short list of words and phrases (again, perhaps twelve or so) that they consider basic and essential to our faith. The bishops, with the help of some professional catechists, could decide on some simple definitions for this short list and ask textbook companies to agree to incorporate them in their series. Such consistency would be a great help for catechists as well as children when changing parishes or textbook series. My only concern about this suggestion is that a dozen words would turn into fifty, and mastering their definitions might take precedence over understanding the concepts they define. The key is to keep the list short and remain true to the catechetical process.

Since the bishops' list is not a reality today, you might consider asking your parish to discern the essentials with care. Prayerfully discerning such a list offers a golden catechetical opportunity. It could be a beneficial exercise for the parish staff or the catechetical team. It might also benefit parents and other adults in the parish. By naming what they think are the essentials of the Catholic faith for children, adults have an opportunity to look at their own belief system, and possibly even relearn some of the basics themselves.

Involving Parish Adults

By addressing the question of Catholic literacy for children, we also have an opportunity to address adult illiteracy. We know adults are much more difficult to reach than children. They learn what they are interested in learning. Experience tells us that adults will often do for their children what they will not do for themselves. So facilitating one or two evenings when parents are invited to talk about developing a strong foundation in basic Catholicism for their children is more likely to draw their interest than offering an adult series on basic doctrine.

One way of facilitating the gathering is to have people pair up or form small groups and decide on a dozen "truths" (words or phrases) they consider essential to the Catholic faith. After a sufficient time, call the groups together to combine their lists. When everyone has had a chance to add ideas, begin whittling the list. Remember to keep the list short and to stick to the fundamentals.

Define the words or phrases in terms simple enough for children to understand. Discuss how the parish, the school or the parish religious education program, along with parents, can help children learn the definitions and, more importantly, grasp the concepts. Remind all concerned that the language of faith is not learned solely in the classroom or from a catechism. Children learn though process, observation, explanation and participation. Mastering the definition comes at the end of a process. The *General Directory* tells us to avoid the risk of mechanical learning, memorization should be "harmoniously inserted into the different functions of learning" and offered as a "syntheses after a process of explanation..." (*GDC* #154).

We must also remember the two other elements that are basic and essential in initiatory catechesis: "the nucleus of Christian experience.... and the most essential evangelical values" (*GDC* #87). Both offer important ways of teaching. Children learn by being involved in what is central to Christian life: our rituals and our values. Children need to hear the words simply defined over and over again, but also they need to learn what they mean through stories, prayers, experiences, rituals and values put into action. In this way the words become theirs.

Varied Approaches

Two words that would be on my short list of fundamentals are *trinity* and *sacraments*. Let me give you some examples of how these words can be understood and the concepts learned with the heart as well as the head.

Trinity. The sisters used to tell us that the Trinity was a mystery; that has not changed. We will never be able to explain our tri-une God to other adults, let alone to children. But learning the names of the "three Persons" is a good way to start. First graders can learn to name the Persons in the Trinity by making the Sign of the Cross and saying the Glory Be. Introducing these prayers by saying, "Let us say our Church's prayer to the Holy Trinity," helps them associate the names of the three Persons with the one triune God. Memorizing these prayers, along with the Our Father, and starting and ending each gathering by using them is a good way to begin.

We also have an obligation to help children experience the triune God and to hear about other people's experiences. The story of creation, nature walks and thanksgiving prayers are simple ways of introducing God the Father, source of all life, who continues to nurture the earth. We also discover each of the divine Persons by reading the stories from Scripture: God's covenant; Jesus' life, death and resurrection; the Spirit's move-ment throughout the early Church.

During a recent parish family retreat, we learned about the Trinity. We started with three rolls of different-colored banner paper (about fifteen feet long and eighteen inches wide)—one sheet for each of the persons in the Trinity. The families talked about God the Father, the source of all life, and listed all the facets of creation for which they were grateful. They talked about Jesus and their favorite stories of his life. They talked about the Holy Spirit and decided on the different words, sym-bols and actions that told them who the Holy Spirit was. They were given time to draw their responses on practice sheets and then on each of the appropriate banners. The families decided which members would work on which banners.

When everyone was finished, we talked about what they

had written and drawn. After the discussion, with the help of the older children, we folded the width of the banners in half and then in half again. This left the banner still fifteen feet long but now only four inches wide. We looked at each of the strips one last time and reminded ourselves that each strip represented one of the three persons in the Holy Trinity. Finally, some of the teens helped me braid the three strips into one band.

We taped the band end to end to form a large circle. The circle became the centerpiece for our closing ritual in which we talked about one God, who, like the circle, had no beginning or end, revealed in three persons. In our parish, the braided circle was used throughout the year to talk about the Trinity, one God revealed in three persons.

Sacrament. I still like to define sacraments the way I was taught: "an outward sign instituted by Christ to give grace." What I like to do is teach children and adults what we mean by "sign" and "grace" and the phrase "instituted by Christ."

After I was enlightened by my experience with my son Peter and the word *sacrament,* I decided to take a new approach to sacraments in the religious education program for which I was responsible. I became the "sacrament lady." Once a year I visited each classroom and talked about the sacraments to the children. I came equipped with my "outward signs" (not just the liturgical ones, but also stop signs, no smoking signs and more) and flash cards. Basically, as "sacrament lady," I became an outward sign of the concept of sacrament.

These sessions were age-appropriate and interactive, with lots of showmanship, especially for the younger children. In the process of explaining sacraments, I also taught the meaning of the words "grace" (walking with God, sharing God's life) and "sin" (choosing to walk away from God, to separate ourselves in big or small ways). Flash cards helped the children learn the words as well as the names of the seven sacraments. By the sixth grade, the youngsters were given an opportunity to present the sacraments in their own way, sometimes helping with the younger grades.

In addition to the yearly visit from the sacrament lady, each class also planned their own liturgy or penance service. They attended a Baptism together or staged their own with a doll. In the meantime, they continued to learn about the sacraments in the same way they always had, from their textbooks and catechists.

My Top Twelve

To spark discussion and debate among religious educators and parish leaders, I present my own short list of the top twelve fundamentals of our faith: (1) Trinity, (2) God's unconditional love, (3) Incarnation, (4) Reign of God, (5) Church, (6) sacrament, (7) Eucharist, (8) grace, (9) sin, (10) Resurrection, (11) prayer, (12) discipleship.

I offer this list as a way you might begin discussion in your own catechetical circle. I encourage you to deliberate on which words you would add or subtract. Better still, come up with your own list. Just remember to keep the list short and basic. Stick to the essential fundamentals.

CHAPTER TEN

Lessons From Russia

The Russian and Lithuanian Ministries of Education a few years ago invited thirty-four Catholic religious educators from the United States and Canada to meet their counterparts in those countries. The letter of invitation said the visit would offer us an opportunity "to network" with our peers in the nations formerly known as the Soviet Union. That it did and more.

Arriving in Moscow on October 2, we were at the Russian circus the next evening when anti-Yeltsin forces began fighting. Gunfire rang out all night. The next morning, as we met with the Russian Minister of Education, we heard helicopters above us and mortar shells going off as the pro-Yeltsin forces stormed the parliament building. Early each day, our guides and interpreters briefed us on the political situation. By the time we left Russia, the Parliament building had been reclaimed, but the political situation was still volatile.

Russia is a beautiful country. Saint Petersburg, in particular, with its Winter Palace and Summer Gardens, its rivers and canals, is surely one of the most beautiful cities in the world. By the end of the trip, however, the consensus among us was that the highlight was neither the history we had witnessed in the making nor the beautiful cities we had seen; it was the people we had met and the stories we had heard.

Three Who Found God

Three individuals especially stand out. All are members of the Association of Scholars, teaching at the Saint Petersburg School of Religion and Philosophy, an independent educational institution founded by several members of the Russian Academy of Sciences.

Our meeting began with brief introductions and preliminary explanations about the school by Natalia, the director. Forty-five minutes into it, one of our delegates asked the teachers present, "How did you become formed in your faith during a time of official atheism?"

Svetlana spoke first. Both her mother and father were physicists, and therefore, she stressed, were naturally atheists. She had been an atheist herself. In her thirties, however, Svetlana began to find God through her work. Her university degrees are in Byzantine art. Faith came to her through the icons and religious artwork she studied and taught. She was baptized at age forty.

Natalia spoke next because she wanted us to know that, although she was a physicist, she was *not* an atheist. In fact, her work in physics led her to believe in God. Science, she came to realize, did not have all the answers. Like many of the Russians we were to meet, Natalia had first been introduced to Christianity by her grandmother, who had taken Natalia to church as a child. Her grandmother had also told her stories of faith.

Vladimir said his parents were both Communists, his father a strong party leader. To please him, Vladimir had spent his boyhood trying to be the best Communist he could be. As a young pioneer, he read and studied everything. At age fourteen, he decided he wanted to be the best Russian he could be, and so started reading Russian literature. There he found God.

Although for decades, faith was a forbidden subject of study and atheism had been taught in every school, some people living under Communism continued to find God. They found God in science. They found God in culture, expressed in the arts, such as painting and literature. And they found God in their homes, as family members kept the traditions and told their own stories of faith to the young.

In Moscow, the minister of education told us that atheism had been taught even in the preschools, which is one of the reasons he felt Communism was ultimately doomed to fail. He said truth would always find a way of winning out, and that God was truth. At one point in our meeting at the Russian Academy of Science, someone asked how much faith and religious knowledge the students brought with them to class. "Anywhere from zero to a hundred," someone answered. But at dinner that night, Vladimir told me that no one comes to them with zero knowledge of God, because God is at the heart of what it means to be Russian.

God is also, of course, at the heart of what it means to be human: We are made in God's image. At our core is the truth, which is why God can be found anywhere. Once God is found and the spark of faith is ignited, however, faith needs to be kindled. In one respect, the faith of the Russians we met was kindled in the same way as is our own, within a community of believers devoted to serve each other and share the message of faith.

Secret Christians

During the Soviet regime, many of the members of the Academy met secretly in each other's cramped apartments, sharing not only their faith but books they somehow smuggled in. They used secret codes in telephoning one another, aware that the next person they called or met might be an informer or a member of the KGB. They risked losing their prestigious jobs as scientists and professors; they risked imprisonment. But the risks didn't stop them. They needed those meetings together; through them their faith and knowledge grew stronger. By 1990, when religious freedom came with Gorbachev's *glasnost*, they were ready to teach others.

I learned many important lessons in those two weeks in Russia and Lithuania, but one of the most significant things I brought back was the reaffirmation of how essential it is for adults to share their faith with each other. The sharing of faith that we saw around kitchen tables in Russia was religious education at its best. It was relational, communal, life-centered and empowering.

Relational

In those Christian circles, each member's life was dependent on the other. Trust was essential not only for their own safety but the safety of those close to them. Those circles existed because of the trust they had for each other and the trust they had in God.

As adults we live our lives in relationship with others and with God. Faith learning has more to do with building and nurturing these trusting relationships than with obtaining information about religion. We come to know God through time spent in prayer and reflection on Scripture *and* through relationships with others. In just such trusting relationships, faith can be challenged to grow.

Forming small Christian faith communities is one way of helping people build relationships; it is not the only way. We need to take every opportunity available to help people connect and network. When planning retreat days and parish missions, it is helpful to include quiet reflection time as well as time for people to get to know each other in formal groups or through informal fellowship. A catechist, by getting to know the people with whom she works, is able to help parishioners with similar interests or needs to come together for networking or support.

Communal

Community sustained the Russian scholars' belief in God. It provided the forum in which each individual articulated religious knowledge and experience, multiplying its effects. The Russian example has counterparts in this country. For too many years U.S. Catholics were brought up with a private notion of faith. Praying with others and talking about one's personal relationship with God has not come easily to many Catholics. We know, however, that faith learning is not simply a matter between one's self and God, that God comes to us in and through community. To experience community, Catholics in the United States have joined thousands of small groups. In parishes, groups often meet for short periods of time (two or three months, for example) to discuss a book or study Scripture.

Some use videotapes as a catalyst for small-group discussion, allowing ample time for groups to process what they have seen and heard.

Many parishes are also involved in organizing small Christian communities, where believers gather over the long term. Most diocesan offices can provide information on national organizations that provide formational help as well as ongoing support for small Christian communities.

Life-Centered

Our Russian friends found God through their work, through their family life and through their personal interests. Then they openly shared their lives and faith experiences with other Christians, helping themselves and each other come to a better understanding of the great mystery that is God.

Because adults are both the learners and the teachers in catechesis, their interests and life situations must always be considered. God is revealed in everyday life, its joys and challenges. Adults find God in their avocations as well as their vocations. By asking adults to reflect on their own issues and interests, parishes help them practice and enlarge their skills in encountering God in daily life. The issues we address in our catechetical programs and the topics we select for small-group sessions must reflect the needs of parishioners.

Empowering

In Russia the act of joining a small group illustrated empowerment. Each meeting gave the members strength to go out and live another day, to return another evening. Many people believe that such small Christian communities contributed to Communism's eventual defeat in the former Soviet Union.

Adult education ought to empower the learner to take responsibility for his or her own faith development. It should also empower adults to look beyond their own personal concerns, becoming disciples to the world. Empowerment involves skills as well as attitudes. Parishes ought to involve as many parishioners as possible as facilitators and group leaders, thus reinforcing the fact that religious education is not just the work of clergy or lay professionals.

In planning religious education programs, the primary purpose is to help individuals develop their own process of critical awareness and careful reflection. A lecture series may be intellectually stimulating, but it puts the learner in a passive position. The more involved the learner is in the process, the greater the opportunity to internalize the message.

Small Communities as Church

I learned much in those two weeks in Russia, not only from the Russian people but also from the other catechetical leaders with me. How good it was to have a group of fellow pilgrims to process the experience! It did not take long for us to become a community. We talked together in pairs and small groups, on the buses and in restaurants as we shared our own stories and the events of two unforgettable weeks. We left Moscow late one evening and drove through dark, almost deserted streets, with armed soldiers at various crossroads. As we rode through the city we sang and prayed together. We harmonized a familiar *Alleluia*. In the simple majesty of that word and melody, and in the company of fellow pilgrims, I remember feeling the comfort of community and the power that is Church.

Part Three
Catechesis, Liturgy and the Liturgical Year

Introduction

> *As for catechesis, it prepares people for full and*
> *active participation in liturgy (by helping them*
> *understand its nature, rituals, and symbols) and*
> *at the same time flows from liturgy, inasmuch as,*
> *reflecting upon the community's experience of*
> *worship, it seeks to relate them to daily life and*
> *to growth in faith.*
> —Sharing the Light of Faith, #113

In the 1979 National Catechetical Directory, *Sharing the Light of Faith*, worship was added to message, community and service as a fourth element of catechesis. Sacraments draw individuals as well as the whole community into more intimate communion with Jesus Christ, the definitive aim of catechesis (*GDC* #80). The liturgical seasons offer the same opportunity.

The sacraments and the liturgical season offer three distinct catechetical moments: defining, preparing for and celebrating the occasion. The first moment, defining, offers an opportunity for parish staff, as well as catechists, to rediscover the meaning of the sacrament or season. Indeed, often the success of preparing for and celebrating a sacrament or season depends on defining beforehand what the experience is about.

In the chapters that follow we look at each of the first sacraments for young people. We will also look at the seasons of Advent and Lent, as well as Liturgy of the Word for children. The suggestions offered for preparing and celebrating each occasion flow from the discussion and definition of what is being celebrated.

Each sacrament and every season poses its own nuance of the God whom we encounter. Each sacrament and every liturgical season offers its own unique symbols, rites and rituals that proclaim who we are as individuals and as a faith community. There are unlimited catechetical opportunities in the process of defining, preparing and celebrating the liturgical life of the parish.

CHAPTER ELEVEN

Liturgy of the Word for Children

Technically, planning Liturgy of the Word for children should probably fall under a parish's liturgical ministry, but in most parishes the responsibility for planning the children's service and training presiders is left to the catechetical leader. When it is, two things should be kept in mind about planning such a liturgy: what *liturgy* is about and what *children* are about.

It's About Liturgy

The most important thing to remember about Liturgy of the Word for children is that it is liturgy, not a time for catechesis. Neither is it a convenient way of "baby-sitting" children beyond nursery age, nor a Sunday Bible School complete with arts and crafts. Rather, it is a time for children to gather, pray together and break open the word of God. Though for children, this is still liturgy, no less sacred, no less estimable than Liturgy of the Word for adults.

In our Church, so steeped in ritual, we do children a disservice if we do not allow them the privilege of participating in our sacred rites. Ritual is important to children. It is comfortable; it is the "known." Try deviating one word from a familiar story and a youngster will call you on it. Rituals offer children a sense of security. We need not fear that by following the rites we will lose our children's attention. As long as we remember to keep things simple and repeat week after week the same procedures and format, the ritual will become their own. Children will enjoy the comfort that ritual provides them in praying with their peers.

It's About Children

Certainly no one would disagree that children are different from adults. Therefore, when we put children in an adult situation and ask them to act appropriately, we need to realize that a certain amount of squirming, talking out loud and leafing through hymnals *is* appropriate. Children do not like to stay still for long, nor do they like to keep quiet. They also have a great need to touch everything near them. When planning Liturgy of the Word for children, involve the children through movement and activity, sound and dialogue and tactile and experiential prayer forms. Invite the children to talk and sing, play musical instruments or dance, for example. Old-fashioned, solemn, hands-folded processing is also a great way to keep children focused and moving from one place to another.

Children are, by their very nature, open to the awesome mystery that is God. They have deep spiritual capacity and often have profound religious experiences. Our job, when planning liturgies or prayer services, is to do our best to create an environment and format that will allow the child's natural capacity for encountering the holy to take over. Ritual is an excellent means. If we pay attention to what captures the child's sense of the sacred, we can allow the rites themselves to speak to and for our young people.

Follow the Rite

Liturgy of the Word has a particular format—a rite that must be followed, if that is what we are going to call the children's worship time together. To meet the specific needs of children, adaptations may be made in accordance with *The Directory for Masses with Children (DMC)*, published in 1973 by the Sacred Congregation for Divine Worship. For example, parts of the Introductory Rite may be omitted or shortened, brief introductory comments are more than appropriate at various times in the service (before the Penitential Rite, readings,

Creed or Prayers of the Faithful, for example), often only two readings are used, and in some cases only the Gospel is read. While you may certainly vary elements within the service, it is important that the basic format always remain evident. In this way, the ritual is sustained and the children can derive all the benefits that come with it.

Setting the Environment

Make sure the space is large enough and comfortable enough for the children who will be gathering. Keep the decor simple and as free from distractions as possible. You might consider these suggestions for creating a suitable and inviting gathering space: a rug or carpet squares to sit on, a table with a candle on which to place the Holy Book, a lectern from which to read, a colored cloth for table or lectern that will change with the liturgical seasons, a simple banner (also in the color of the liturgical season).

Remember that children are very much in tune with their senses. Use water occasionally for a blessing rite at the beginning of the celebration. If possible, offer them an opportunity to put their hands in it—to bless themselves and each other. Call their attention to the sound the water makes while it is being poured and as the presider invokes a blessing. Also try to incorporate some periods of silence, though these must be brief to begin with. Silence is an important part of the prayer experience for both adults and children, and even the very young can learn to close their eyes and be still for a few seconds.

Assembling the Children

There are several ways to gather the youngsters. In some parishes the children go directly to their own assembly space. In other parishes the children sit in the pews with their parents until the appointed time. The advantage of the latter is that when it is time to join parents for the Liturgy of the Eucharist, children know exactly where to find them.

Children can be led out of the general assembly space in

various ways. In one parish, the commentator invites the children to follow the candle bearers (two youngsters who are standing at the front of the middle aisle) before the priest processes into the church. In another parish, the children remain present through the opening song. Then the presider for children's liturgy is called forward, given the children's lectionary and charged with responsibility for breaking open the word. The presider calls the children to the front and leads them out, carrying the Holy Book held high.

One of my favorite experiences of gathering youngsters for the Liturgy of the Word took place at a parish I worked in several years ago, where religious education classes were held on Sunday mornings between Masses. At the later Mass, the children in church were led out to the Liturgy of the Word by one candle bearer, while another candle bearer walked down the halls of the classrooms. He or she knocked on each classroom door and then opened it. The candle bearers always said, "It is time to hear the word of God. Come and follow me." At that, the children were told to stop whatever they were doing. They were to leave books open and pencils out, and follow the candle bearer silently out of the room. I loved to watch that quiet procession of youngsters going from room to room. It was a great way to impress on them the importance of liturgy and God's Word. And I know that the children enjoyed the drama of dropping everything, and sometimes leaving their teacher in mid-sentence. After the Liturgy of the Word, those children who were not attending the eucharistic celebration, returned to class and were later dismissed from there. The others joined the adults in the larger church and gathered their belongings after Mass.

Introductory Rites

If the children are going directly to the assembly space, an opening song is certainly appropriate. Music is such a natural way for children to celebrate that, even if the youngsters have already sung an opening song with the general assembly, you may still want to lead them in another song as they begin their own liturgy. The presider then greets the children. You might plan a short penitential rite (in the presider's own words or the more traditional Lord, Have Mercy) and possibly the Gloria. The presider then says a short opening prayer and invites the children to listen to God's word. A few comments before the reading are appropriate to set tone, place and background.

Proclaiming the Word

A child or teenager may proclaim the first reading. Make sure the reader is chosen carefully and has had time to prepare. The reading needs to be loud enough, slow enough and clear enough to capture the attention of even the youngest child. A responsorial psalm or an alleluia may be sung between readings. Some parishes, rather than reading the Scripture of the day, dramatize it or show a video or slide presentation of it instead. While these may be excellent ways of helping the children focus on the readings, I suggest first proclaiming the word from the lectionary and then following it with the dramatization or videotape.

Breaking Open the Word

Following the Scripture, the presider may offer a few brief comments (emphasis on brief). If the gathering of children is large, you may divide them by age or by number. Or the gathering may simply remain large. In any case, it is important to engage the young people in dialogue by asking relevant questions and listening well. Ask the children what they heard. What was the Scripture about? What was their favorite part? What do they think Jesus is asking them to do? The idea is to help them make the reading relevant to their own lives. This is not the time for instruction or teaching or for head learning. Rather this ought to be a life-giving "experience."

While Liturgy of the Word should never be confused with arts-and-crafts time, it is true that the best way to engage young children in dialogue is through the act of cutting and pasting things together. Just make sure that the focus of the activity is on hearing and celebrating the Scripture and not on creating busy work. The *Directory* suggests using pictures prepared by the children to illustrate the homily or to give a visual dimension to the prayers of the faithful (*DMC* #36).

Profession of Faith and Prayers of Intercession

The Liturgy of the Word ends with the children reciting the Creed and offering the Prayers of Intercession. While some parishes prefer to have their youngsters remain in small groups for these prayers, I like reassembling them so they can say the prayers all together. In this way the move back to a larger assembly is more gradual, and the children are given the opportunity to hear more voices in petition and response. If the Creed is going to be recited, you may want to have the words written on poster board in large print so that children have no trouble reading them. The presider can lead the Prayers of the Faithful, asking the youngsters to offer their own prayers.

Timing at this point is important. Ask one of the ushers to keep the presider informed of the progress of the adult assembly. When the usher judges that the priest is nearing the end of his homily, it is time for the presider to go to each group and call them back. It is always a good idea to have a song, prayer or story ready in case the homily goes longer than usual. The children process back into church during the Offertory.

Training Presiders and Facilitators

One of the most difficult concepts I have found in training presiders and facilitators is to convince them they are leading prayer, not teaching. Their job is to help facilitate the child's encounter with community and with God. Presiders need to remain peripheral to the experience, not central. Their words and voices should lead and not impose. Another difficult concept to convey is that liturgy is a celebration. As a children's celebration, there should, at times, be an atmosphere of respectful playfulness. Just as there is time for silence and time for solemn processions, there should also be time for smiles and happy faces, particularly during the greeting and homily, and certainly in the music, singing and dancing.

Perhaps the best way to help adults understand these two concepts is by holding a full-day workshop and retreat. Allow the participants to talk about and experience for themselves the difference between prayer time, learning time and party time. Make sure you create separate environments for each. Use ritual and symbols. Involve adults themselves in tactile experiences, as well as in scriptural dialogue with each other, to see that in celebrating with each other they are celebrating with God.

I know from my own experience that most people who facilitate the small groups are much more comfortable if they have materials to use with youngsters. Certainly, publishers offer a variety of lectionary-based materials. As long as these materials are used as a resource to focus on celebrating and integrating the message and not teaching it or imposing it, they are fine. Too often, however, they are used as study pages. And in most cases, far more material is offered than can be used during the worship time. Sometimes this material works best as reference material for the facilitator and take-home activities for the children.

Hearing the Message

While the Liturgy of the Word is not supposed to be a time for catechesis, it will still be a learning experience. No youngster will walk away from the thirty or so minutes at liturgy without having learned something. Hopefully they will not only carry with them the message of that week's Gospel but also walk away knowing that they are respected and loved by God and by the parish community of which they are a valued member.

CHAPTER TWELVE

Confirmation:
Catechesis for Early Teens

M ost things, it seems, were simpler when I was a youngster. That was certainly true about Confirmation. I remember only three things about the day I received the sacrament: the not-so-gentle slap that made me a soldier of Christ, the bishop pointing to me and asking why God had made me and the fact that I was allowed to wear nylon stockings, just like a grown-up woman, for the first time.

Confirmation, like so much in the Church at that time, was well defined: It was the sacrament through which the Holy Spirit came to make a person a strong and perfect Christian and a soldier of Christ. Confirmation enabled us to profess the faith (hence, the need to memorize the *Baltimore Catechism*) and strengthened us against the dangers to salvation. It was also a sacrament of maturity. While the Church may have used oil to leave that indelible mark, for most of us girls in the sixth grade, not having to wear anklets was the true sign that we were grown-ups in the Church.

Things are not so easily defined today. Indeed, Confirmation seems to be a sacrament still in search of a theology. While most people agree that it is *not* a sacrament of maturity, theologians and liturgists continue to discuss its purpose and meaning, arguing about its proper position among the Sacraments of Initiation. Even Catholics in the pews are entering the debate, questioning why, for example, the seven-year-olds being baptized are also being confirmed while others of their classmates have to wait six or more years to receive "the fullness of the Holy Spirit."

While a number of dioceses have begun celebrating the Sacrament of Confirmation with children in the primary grades, the majority of dioceses still celebrate it with older children. This has been my own experience. Consequently, I have decided against joining the debate over the who, what and when of Confirmation, in favor of writing about one particular "how." In the small urban parishes where I ministered for six years, I helped prepare young teens for Confirmation through a teens and elders program (described in chapter Twenty-Four, "A Pastoral Approach," page 173). Here, however, I outline the process used in a large suburban parish where I worked for my first ten years as a director of religious education. Both programs involved youngsters in their early teens; both were designed to help them understand and experience what Christian community is all about.

Ninth Graders: Experiencing Christian Community

During my first year as a director of religious education, our spring Confirmation date was cancelled when the archbishop was reassigned. The occasion offered us an opportunity to move the reception of the sacrament from eighth grade to ninth grade, which turned out to be a blessing in disguise. We scheduled a new date for later in the fall and designed a short, concentrated, two-and-a-half-month program to refresh the memories of our teens. The program turned out to be so successful that we continued to confirm ninth graders and followed the same basic structure for the next nine years.

Celebrating the sacrament in the ninth grade offered two advantages. We stressed to both the parents and the youngsters that Confirmation was not the end of their involvement in the parish, but a new beginning. It also gave us an opportunity to foster teen involvement in the parish through a peer ministry group. The effect was that even those youngsters whose parents had "made" them come to Confirmation preparation remained active in the parish youth group throughout their high school years.

The Program

The program itself was simple. We met every Sunday after-noon for two-and-a-half months. In addition, each teen was required to participate in three service projects and to attend an overnight retreat. Much of the program's success is attributable to another factor as well: We engaged several college students to serve as catechists and mentors to the teens. These mentors were present throughout the entire process—from the first meeting, through the retreat and service projects, to the actual Confirmation rite. Although the first year began with only four college students, by the tenth year we had enlisted more than a dozen. In the later years of the program, many of the college mentors had gone though the Confirmation program them-selves as teens. (We also involved older high school students to work as small-group facilitators.)

The Retreat

Early in September we scheduled an overnight retreat at the parish. The youngsters slept on meeting-room floors, prepared their food in the church kitchen and spent some special time alone in the quiet darkness of the church. For that two-day overnight retreat, the building was theirs. Through various activities, prayer services and witness talks they were able to claim their ownership of the church in a broader sense.

The retreat ended with an enrollment ceremony at one of the regular weekend liturgies. There the Confirmation candi-dates were formally presented to the parish community, who blessed them and pledged to support them. The retreat was an important beginning. It provided an opportunity for the young people to bond with one another and set in place an enjoyable pattern of working, learning, praying and playing together.

At a prayer service that weekend, the teens were told to pick out a place in church—in the pews or on the floor or wher-ever they wanted—to be their "spot." There were only two rules: I had to be able to see them and they could not be within six feet of anyone else. They would return to their "quiet spots" several times in the weeks that followed. To this spot they would bring their parents, and later their sponsors, for some one-on-one discussion during the parent meetings and before Confirmation practice.

The Weekly Meetings

The two-hour Sunday afternoon meetings went by quickly as the teens moved between small-class to large-group settings. Each meeting, they spent one half hour in small groups learning about sacraments with a special emphasis on Confirmation, and another half hour reviewing Scripture and doctrine. The collegiate catechists and high school facilitators gave credence to faith issues and made learning fun. The last hour was spent in the large group, where the candidates worked on various activities and projects, designed to help them get to know each other on a deeper level and to build trust and community.

We also spent that last hour on tasks such as planning the Confirmation liturgy and designing a group banner. The Confirmation banner took several weeks of planning. The eight-foot banner was to hang in the sanctuary during their Confirmation and then be moved to the fellowship hall for the reception. A special place was reserved for it right under the hall's clock. Banners from earlier Confirmation classes had been hanging in the hall since the group's first meeting, with that empty space waiting. The youngsters knew that next September their banner would be hanging there among the rest. Confirmation banners became a tradition at the parish, decorating the hall from September to Thanksgiving. The parish enjoyed watching its young people of high school or college age as they stopped on their way through the hall Sunday mornings, to find their initials on the banner their class had made years before.

Service Opportunities

Another parish tradition grew out of the Confirmation preparation—the annual ham-and-eggs breakfast. Each year on a particular Sunday in October the Confirmation class prepared and served an elaborate breakfast after each of the Masses. Parishioners were charged a nominal fee, with special family rates. Candidates chose the Mass at which they wanted to work, and everyone had a voice in deciding which charity would receive the money earned.

They also had a choice about the second service project: Sometimes it entailed working at a soup kitchen or planning a children's Halloween party for the parish. Each year the projects differed. Whatever project candidates chose, they would be working with other candidates, college students and their high school supporters. Working together on the service projects helped them build community.

The final service project was to be done in secret. Two weeks before Confirmation, while spending some quiet time in the church, the candidates were asked to decide on some service they would perform in the week ahead. They were to keep the deed "between themselves and God." We never asked the candidates what they were going to do or whether they had done it. So there was no way of knowing how many teens would take this project seriously. From comments made in the weeks that followed, however, we learned that for many of them, the "secret service" had been a positive experience.

Developing Trust

One reason the groups bonded so well was that the rules of the process were laid down at the opening talk. The talk was the same each year, and I gave it. There were only two rules the youths needed to abide by whenever we were together: (1) They would respect each other, and (2) they would respect the church in which they met. That meant, for example, that there was to be no gossiping or snickering behind people's backs. They did not have to agree with each other, but they would respect each other.

I told them that if they could not follow those rules, they could still be confirmed, but not prepared with the group. Rather, their parents would be given material to work with them at home. The intention was that for two and a half months they would have a place to come where they could be themselves and feel accepted. That was what we promised them and that is what we worked hard to deliver.

In the final weeks of their preparation they were given a packet of papers in which every parish ministry was listed, along with an explanation of how a young person could become more involved in the larger parish. The young people were invited to become eucharistic ministers and lectors. They were asked to help the men's club with the annual picnic. They were invited to become aides in the religious education program or helpers at Bible School. The candidates filled out the volunteer forms for the various ministries they selected.

A Taste of Community

When teens are confirmed, the rite is usually understood as a celebration of the final step of their initiation into the larger Christian community. It seems appropriate, then, to design a catechetical process that gives them a taste of what a Christian community should be like, along with an invitation to become more involved in the parish.

CHAPTER THIRTEEN

First Communion:
A Teachable Moment

A bout my Confirmation, I remember three things, but I remember only two things about my first Communion: a vase filled with red roses and a torn slip. The roses—a whole dozen—were a gift from my godfather. The best gift I had ever received, they made me feel extraordinarily special. The torn slip is a story that fits in later. Most Catholics have clear memories of their first Communion and, probably tucked away somewhere, a photograph of themselves on that day. My family album shows four generations of first communicants, a testimony that my family, like so many other Catholic families, viewed first Eucharist as a major event. With a little planning, this family/church celebration can be a teachable moment, not only for the second graders involved but their parents and the whole parish as well.

First Communion Is About Initiation

The preparation period gives us as catechists an opportunity to remind the congregation that first Communion is a Sacrament of Initiation. Like Baptism and Confirmation, it is celebrated by the entire Church, represented by the local parish.

A simple enrollment ceremony at the Sunday liturgy when the children begin preparing serves as an effective reminder of its significance. Ask parents and children to meet a few minutes before the weekend Mass they usually attend. Have name tags ready for the children. Instruct the parents and children on the simple responses they will be asked to make, and ask them to sit where they usually do for liturgy. After the homily the parents stand and the presider asks if they will do their best to help prepare their youngsters for the sacrament. When the parents consent and are blessed by the congregation, the children stand and make their promises. The people in the pews are also asked if they are ready to support the parents, catechists and children. The catechists are called forward to affirm their readiness and finally, the children are called forward by name. The catechists who are still at the front of the church remove each child's name tag and place it on an appropriately decorated banner (or poster board). The congregation blesses the catechists and children. The whole ritual takes no more than five minutes and reminds the church gathered of their responsibility in the faith life of the parish young people.

First Communion, too, should be celebrated during the Sunday liturgy, preferably for small groups of children, allowing them to feel special and the parishioners to find enough seats. For the entrance rite, consider having the children join the procession, each with their lighted baptismal candle, pausing to "renew" (that is, say aloud publicly) their baptismal promises. Many parishes plan a reception afterwards, encouraging all present to meet and congratulate the children and their families.

First Communion Is About Belonging

Inviting youngsters to receive the Body and Blood of Christ incorporates them more fully into the worshiping community. Part of our ministry as catechists is to help young people experience the feeling of being welcomed into that community. Here are a few practical suggestions:

• Hang the children's names and pictures in a prominent place in the parish. It will help them understand the importance of the coming occasion and will help the parish get to know them.

• Present the children with a cross or badge with their names on it at the beginning of the year. Ask them to wear it to church each Sunday and encourage parishioners to greet them by name.

- Send each child a letter the week before first Communion. Children love receiving mail. Use simple words and big letters, a message a child (in many parishes it is a second grader) can read without adult help. Express how happy you are that the youngster is finally old enough to come to Jesus' table. Mention how proud the whole parish is that the child is to receive first Communion.

- Include the older children in the parish. For example, at the beginning of Lent, give each youngster in grades three and up the name of a second grader to pray for. During one class, ask them to make a card wishing the first communicant well. As they work, ask about their own first Communion. How did they prepare for the day? What happened on the day? Such memories might remain vivid if children were invited to recount their first Communion year after year. Finally, ask the older children to present their custom-made greeting cards to the younger children on their first Communion day.

Senior parishioners might also enjoy making something special for the first communicants—small wooden crosses or badges, a crocheted gift, or silk corsages and boutonnieres. Be sure to acknowledge any contribution the seniors make so that the youngsters and congregation are both aware of it. It is an effective way of linking generations.

First Communion Is About Solidarity

The Eucharist celebrates the oneness of all people in Christ and with one another. As communicants, Christians are no longer young or old, rich or poor, but as Christ's body and God's people, are indivisible. The Eucharist is rightly called Communion.

A way religious educators can help children and adults experience solidarity is to have the parochial school children and those in religious education prepare for and celebrate first Communion together. Many parishes also sponsor a pre-

Communion "Jesus Day," that is, a Saturday morning or afternoon retreat for all parish second graders, planned and executed by parents from both the school and religious education program.

At each first Communion liturgy, reserve as many pews up front as necessary and invite the children to sit with their families. (Each family gets its own pew.) The first communicant sits on the aisle beside mom, dad and the rest of the family—grandparents, aunts or uncles, sisters or brothers and close friends. Other parishioners fill in any extra spaces. Such seating allows parents who are separated or divorced to find a comfortable place to sit within the family grouping.

Invite the children to come around the altar for the Eucharistic Prayer, offering them a chance to be up close, right next to the priest, watching his every move and listening to the words of the prayer. I have heard many adult members of the congregation say how refreshing it is to see such innocent young faces around the altar and how it brings back memories of their own first Communion day.

Consider directing the youngsters to hold hands during the Our Father. At the sign of peace send them out into the congregation to share the peace of Christ with a warm smile and a handshake. You might even assign a few youngsters to each aisle to make sure they reach as many parishioners as possible. It is delightful to watch the children's smiles spread throughout the congregation. Instruct them to return to their family pew when they hear the Lamb of God and give a big hug to their own family members.

Guide the youngsters to receive Communion *not as a subgroup, lined up with their peers*, but to take their turn along with everyone else. Make sure the ushers understand what is to take place and why so they will be prepared to orchestrate the Communion line, pew after pew, just as at any Sunday liturgy. Receiving the Eucharist with and among the whole community signifies the child's Communion with the adult Church.

Be forewarned! The congregation might find this unusual arrangement uncomfortable, and some ushers have even found it difficult *not* to group the first communicants together at the head of the line. Avoid confusion by explaining briefly in the bulletin or before Mass the reasons behind the action.

First Communion Is About Mystery

At rehearsal, I ask each group of children to stand in a circle around the altar. I speak in a hushed tone. "This is a special table. We don't put our arms or any objects on it, we show special respect for it," I begin. I ask them to tell me what happens here. Then I explain that as the priest leads the congregation's prayer, he takes the bread and wine in his hands and repeats the words that Jesus said so many years ago: This is my body, this is my blood. "We Catholics believe that it isn't bread and wine anymore, but what is it?" I ask. "It's Jesus," they all answer. "Yes. We don't understand how, but we believe that it is. Now you, too, are coming to this table, joining in a sacramental meal Catholics have been celebrating for thousands of years."

Because love, solidarity and belonging are deeply felt but difficult to express, we need the sacraments—effecting the grace they signify. Words are spoken, the bread is broken and the Body and Blood of Christ are received. We know the what, the when and the why of this sacrament, but not the how. We teach children about matter and form and retell the story of the Last Supper, but *how* God's great love transcends time and substance to unite us as Christ's body will always be a mystery.

First Communion Is About Love

The Eucharist is always a powerful sacrament of God's great love. First Communion offers parents, especially, an opportunity to make sure their child feels extraordinarily loved. Parents should be involved as much as possible in the sacramental preparation of their children. Some parishes separate the preparation from the regular religious education program to facilitate a home-study program or a family-based program instead. In both cases parents usually end up learning more than their children.

Parent sacramental preparation meetings, then, are essential. First Communion is an appropriate time to evangelize parents, especially those who may not have attended church for a while. When children reach the age of seven their parents are often at a point in their lives, established in their jobs and settled into family life, where they are ready to rethink their involvement in parish life. This gives the parish staff an opportunity to update the parent's theology and gently invite them back home.

When speaking to parents, it helps to bear in mind that covering the nuts and bolts of the celebration is secondary to talking about a loving God, Jesus, the importance of a supportive community and the awesome responsibility of parents in handing on the faith to their children. Include no preaching and no guilt trips, just a reality check on what God and Church are all about.

Schedule the last sacramental preparation meeting just before the children's only rehearsal—the Saturday morning before they are to receive Communion. Each group practices separately, so you are able to work with a small group of parents each time.

Parents are required to accompany their children to the rehearsal. They are asked to pay close attention, for they will have to help their child know when to stand, come forward or go to the back of church to bring up the gifts. It is important to stress the fact that the Mass is not a performance; it is a celebration with children. Mistakes may occur, but parents can assure their youngsters that everything is okay.

A Communion Story

At the rehearsal, while the children are out of the room practicing a song or learning to line up, I tell the parents the story of the torn slip.

On my first Communion day, I dressed early and looked dazzling in my white dress, veil, stockings and shoes. Unfortunately, I was a tomboy, the middle daughter of three.

Mother used to say she could send me out the front door as neat as a pin, but by the time I got to the back door I looked like a war orphan. First Communion day was no exception. In the time it took my mother to put a coat and hat on my little sister, I had managed to tear my slip. It hung two inches below my dress. In the taxi on the way to church, my mother mended the slip and scolded me. It was not a happy memory.

Years later, a parent myself, I noticed that I had inherited my mother's tendency occasionally to overreact under pressure. At an early age my children learned to scatter when I was getting ready for out-of-town company. On one such occasion I found myself scolding my own seven-year-old son for some minor misdemeanor the morning of his first Communion. I was graced with the memory of the torn slip. And so instead of making one more salad or cleaning some obscure corner of the house, I took my little boy aside and quietly spent time talking with him about his day.

After sharing this story, I suggest the parents take a few quiet moments to focus on the significance of the occasion: Their child is about to receive Communion. I recommend that they spend one-on-one quality time with their child, perhaps bring out the Baptism pictures, snuggle close and tell their child how much he or she is loved. The best way for children to experience God's love is to experience parental love first. Encountering Christ in the mysteries of consecrated bread and wine will be more significant if they have first experienced Christ in the flesh and blood of someone they love.

CHAPTER FOURTEEN

First Penance:
Celebrating Reconciliation

A s a group of us talked about preparing youngsters for first Reconciliation, a priest in the group said that when parents are invited to receive the sacrament with their children, they often admit it has been a long time—eighteen or twenty years—since *their* last confession. "In effect," he went on, "many of those parents are probably receiving their *second* Reconciliation as their children are receiving their *first*."

None of us around the table that day were surprised. We were all aware that the sacrament that had once been a hallmark of Catholicism had somehow been reduced to less than second-class status. Even some of the most faithful Catholics avoid this sacrament. And parents who are the most eager for their second grader to receive "Confession" have sometimes not been near the sacrament themselves for years. It would seem that the average Catholic's attitude toward the Sacrament of Reconciliation or Penance could be described as anywhere from uncomfortable to downright hostile.

The question for religious educators is: How can we help restore the Sacrament of Penance to its appropriate place? I am certainly not advocating a return to the weekly ritual of standing in line for Saturday afternoon confessions. Nor do I believe we can talk people into changing long-held attitudes toward the sacrament. I do think, however, that if care is taken when religious educators first present the sacrament, we might be able to help the next generation of Catholics have a healthier regard for it, and meanwhile, might help this generation of adult Catholics to rethink their attitudes about it. Perhaps by carefully planning the catechesis and celebration of the sacrament, we might be able to lay some groundwork to help the Sacrament of Penance find its rightful place in the lives of today's Catholics.

Whom Do We Catechize?

Obviously the children who will be receiving the sacrament for the first time need to be introduced to what the Rite of Reconciliation is all about. But there are other people who may also need to be catechized. In effect, any adult who will be involved in the child's catechesis and will, therefore, have a part in shaping the child's attitudes toward Penance should be reintroduced to the sacrament.

Parents are the first people we need to reach. As in all areas of faith formation, we will have more success in effecting the faith life of children if their parents are a part of the process. Whatever approach your parish takes—parents preparing their children at home or parents and children catechized at the same time or children learning about the sacrament in parochial schools and religious programs—you need to talk to the parents *before* they talk to their children.

Directors of religious education also need to spend some time with parish catechists before they introduce the sacrament to our youngsters. (A catechist may be a volunteer in your parish program or a teacher in the parochial school.) Make sure that any adult who will be talking about the Sacrament of Penance to children attends the parent meeting, or schedule a special session for catechists to talk about the sacrament. Even when textbooks or family catechetical series do a great job of presenting the sacrament in a positive, life-giving way, catechists, without meaning to do so, can still color a child's viewpoint with words or examples that reflect their own, perhaps less positive, attitudes.

What Do We Say?

We begin with a person's own experience, connect that

experience to what we hope to teach, provide the appropriate theological and scriptural references and then invite each person to apply the teaching to his or her own life. This is simply sound catechetical process. Now we need to fill in the blanks.

Their own experience. Sometimes the first step in changing one's attitude is to name the attitude and try to figure out how it came about in the first place. At the beginning of your meeting, consider giving adults an opportunity to talk about how they relate to the Sacrament of Penance. Ask them to share their own experiences if they wish. This is probably best done in small groups or in triads. Ask non-Catholic parents to reflect on their own view of the Catholic sacrament in light of what they know—whether from movies or television or from what they have heard from Catholic spouses, friends or others. After a little while, ask if anyone would like to share with the larger group.

Connecting to a new idea. It is said that history is a great teacher, and in the case of the Sacrament of Penance I have found this especially true. After giving people a chance to reflect on their own experiences, try offering a brief presentation on the history of Reconciliation in the Catholic Church. This historical background can sometimes serve as a bridge to a broader, healthier understanding of the sacrament.

Let parents and catechists know that you are hoping to create a positive experience of the sacrament for today's children, but you will need their help to do this. Point out how easily children form opinions by picking up the subtle messages of adults, both spoken and unspoken. Ask those who have had a negative experience of the sacrament to make a conscious effort not to pass on that negative impression. Explain that the Second Vatican Council changed the Rite of Penance after studying its history and reflecting on Scripture and Jesus' gift of Reconciliation. Changing the rite, however, could not erase personal memories or inherited attitudes toward the gift of Reconciliation. Explain your hope that as they listen to the history of the sacrament both parents and catechists will begin to rethink their own attitudes.

By reflecting on the beginnings of this sacrament, adults often realize for the first time the communal dimension that is so important. The Church's earliest experiences teach us that when we fail to live up to our Christian commitment, we are failing the community, not merely ourselves. Therefore, we need to reconcile not only with God but also with the community. The priest forgives not only in God's name but also serves as a representative of the body of Christ. He forgives for the community, on its behalf.

We also learn something about change and our Church when we study the history of this sacrament. When we look at the various stages the sacrament has undergone through the centuries, we are also reminding people that our Church is a living institution, and, like all living things, is also subject to change. Our sacramental system has and will continue to develop, just as our theology and traditions have and still are.

Scripture and theology. After answering any questions and listening to responses, you might suggest taking a closer look at the Sacrament of Penance itself. One way of beginning is by talking about what a sacrament is. Emphasize sacrament as a visible sign of God. And the sacraments (plural) as seven specific signs of times when the Church recognizes and celebrates God with and in the life of a Christian as part of the body of Christ. The sacraments recognize an all-loving God who is always reaching out to us. In the Sacrament of Penance the community celebrates those times in our lives when we recognize our failures and reach back for God's embrace through Christ's body, the Church. Penance is the Sacrament of Reconciliation, it is the embrace of the father and his prodigal son (Luke 15:11-32).

In that parable, much took place before that embrace. The younger son saw his sin, repented, turned around and headed home. None of those actions was easy for the young man, nor are they easy for us. Nevertheless, they will always be a part of our Christian journey. We are regularly in need of repentance and conversion. The more we come to know the goodness of God, the more clearly we see ourselves. Only God is perfect; we make mistakes, big ones and small ones. We sin. Like the prodigal, we need to see our sins, repent and turn around, mindful of the embrace that is always awaiting us.

Applying to one's life. Ask the adults who are gathered to take some quiet time to reflect on what they have heard about the Sacrament of Reconciliation. You might give them one or two questions to use for their reflection: What was the most significant thing you heard during our talk on the Sacrament of Penance? In what way or ways, if any, has your view of the sacrament changed since the beginning of the meeting? After sufficient time, ask the adults to get together with the people in their earlier small group and talk about their reflections.

If the adults you are working with are parents, you will want to spend some additional time suggesting ways they can help their children develop a healthy conscience, as well as model the gift of forgiveness and reconciliation within their family. Numerous resources are available on both subjects. Children's textbooks usually provide family pages or an accompanying parent booklet offering such help. Following are examples of some key issues parents will need to be reminded of:

- A child's conscience develops gradually, just like the rest of the child. Do not expect a six- or seven-year-old to have a highly developed sense of right and wrong.

- A child's moral code is more likely to be determined by how a parent acts than by what the parent says.

- Parents need to help children reflect on their own actions, learning to distinguish between mistakes and deliberate, hurtful acts. Parents need to ask children the "why" behind their actions.

- It is essential that parents make it clear that while they may disapprove of a child's *action*, they do not disapprove of the *child*.

- Parents need to teach their children to say they are sorry and to make amends. They also need to let their child hear them, as parents, say they are sorry and see parents make amends.

- Finally, the way we celebrate the Sacrament of Reconciliation will say a lot about what we believe the sacrament to be.

Celebrating the Sacrament

Since this sacrament celebrates the Church's experience of an all-loving, merciful God, it would seem appropriate to celebrate with the larger community. It is appropriate to invite the "whole parish family" to attend, so announcements should be put in parish bulletins. Music, Scripture and quiet time for reflection can all be a part of the evening.

One of the best approaches I have seen to individual absolution is to invite participants to approach the sanctuary (just as they do when they receive the Eucharist, the primary sacrament of forgiveness). The priest waits there where the penitent presents herself or himself, tells what sin is being repented of, listens to a sentence or two of comforting words and then experiences the laying on of hands as the symbolic embrace of God's forgiveness and the forgiveness of the community.

Afterward, consider hosting a party. Even if the celebration takes place during Lent, offer cookies and punch or pizza and pop, plus music and laughter. Short of the fatted calf, a party will help carry through the idea that this sacrament, like all of the sacraments, is a joyful event, a celebration.

A Brief Historical Sketch of the Sacrament's Development

Public Penance
—second through fifth centuries

Sin is understood as an affront to the community. Serious sins of public scandal mean "excommunication" from the Christian community. Lesser sins of weakness are taken care of through prayer and reconciliation at Sunday Eucharist. Serious sins of public scandal, apostasy, murder, adultery, for example, can only be reconciled—and communion restored—after years of public penance. The sacrament is administered by the bishop in three stages and can be received only once in a lifetime.

Tarrifed penance
—sixth through eleventh centuries
Sin becomes a private matter, an understanding that evolved in the Celtic monasteries and was introduced to Europe by Irish monks, who were ministers but not necessarily clergy. The confessor is seen as a spiritual director. Confessing one's sin is secondary to the penitential effort that leads to reconciliation. Penance is less severe, but explicitly set down. Each sin has a corresponding penance.

Sacrament of "Confession"
—twelfth century until Vatican II
Reconciliation becomes "Confession." Absolution is given *before* penance. The priest becomes a judge. Telling specific sins becomes important: How many? What kind? The private nature of Confession leads to a popular understanding of sin as individualistic, a matter between the person and God. The rite and ideas of private Sacrament of Penance remain unchanged from the fifteenth century—from the Council of Trent to the Second Vatican Council in the 1960s.

Sacrament of Reconciliation
—1965 to present
Vatican II introduces three new rites and a

renewed attitude toward the sacrament. Historical research gives new insights unavailable at the time of Trent. It reinstates the communal nature of the sacrament through suggested rites and settings. The Church uses the term "Reconciliation" to remind the faithful of the positive nature of the sacrament.

CHAPTER FIFTEEN

A Merry Advent and a Happy Christmas

E very fall it happens suddenly: the realization that it is *that* time of year again. Halloween is past, Thanksgiving is here and the entire country seems to be wrapped in red and green. Christmas is on the way.

It is funny how we Christians have left our mark on the culture. In stores and schools, on neighborhood streets and in public libraries, people market our holy day (marketing being the operative word). Every year the whole joyful, merry season seems to become less Christian and more commercial. The media has done a great job of capturing everyone's attention; now we Christians just have to figure out how we can make the Christmas hype work for us. How can we turn the Christmas countdown into a teachable moment?

What to Do?

There are two things we need to do. First, and most important, we need to clarify what the whole season is about. Second, we need to remind the people in our parishes that the end of November marks the beginning of Advent and not the Christmas season. Perhaps one way to accomplish the first objective is to pay more attention to the second.

People need to be reminded that the Christmas season does not begin when Santa arrives at the mall. Rather, it begins on December 25 and goes on, as the song says, for twelve days. Each year, it seems, we need to clarify that the four weeks before Christmas make up Advent, a whole different season

with its own special color and style. Advent is a time of antici-
pation and preparation, which means that basically, the com-
mercialized idea of getting ready for Christmas is, at least, on
target.

A Family Advent Rally

Publishers put out many and varied Advent booklets with
helpful home activities for families. Why not plan a parish
potluck supper to share some of those ideas?

Hands-on activities are always a good idea when working
with both adults and children. If you have a space large enough,
arrange a number of different tables with a variety of projects
from which participants can choose. Have printed instructions
at each table or find a volunteer willing to explain what is to be
done. Ask the adults to work with the smaller children, allowing the older children to work on their own. Make sure to give
families the option of working together as a unit.

Making Advent wreaths from fresh or artificial greens is
always a good project. You might also have participants put
together an Advent calendar to take home or make special
Christmas cards to send grandparents from the whole family.
You might even suggest that they send out their Christmas
cards late in December so that people receive them after the
twenty-fifth, during the real Christmas season! End your time
together with a prayer service, emphasizing what Advent is all
about. Encourage parents and children to spend some time
together during the weeks and days ahead in quiet activities
and prayer. Send them home with plenty of activity ideas.

You could also bring the parish together to collect canned
goods and other foodstuffs. Spend the evening boxing family-
sized dinners to be distributed to those in need. When the work
is finished, divide into small intergenerational groupings and
exchange favorite Christmas traditions or special Christmas
memories. Remind participants that Christmas does not end at
midnight on the twenty-fifth. Encourage them to plan now to
celebrate the season into the new year.

An Advent Party for the Whole Parish

Consider holding a New Year's Eve party the night before the first Sunday in Advent to celebrate the new liturgical year. Since this often falls on the Saturday of the Thanksgiving weekend, you might suggest a potluck supper where parishioners can share their tasty leftovers. The party becomes another opportunity to remind the parish of what Advent is. Send them home with materials to help them celebrate Advent and to enjoy an extended Christmas season.

No Christmas Parties During Advent

Plan all parish celebrations—including classroom parties, staff parties and faculty parties—to take place after Christmas Day. Many parishes that have tried this find that people prefer coming together after the cookies are baked and the gifts have been wrapped, given and unwrapped. After Christmas Day, the ambience is much calmer. Expect a better turnout, too, than when parties are held before December 25.

A Parish Children's Party

At the large suburban parish where I first started working as a director of religious education, an after-Christmas day children's party is still an ongoing tradition. The idea began as a way to bring the children who attended Catholic schools together with those in the parish religious education program. As Advent approached, we decided to plan a Christmas party the children would not only enjoy but remember. We planned an old-fashioned birthday party with games and prizes, presents and balloons.

Invitations were sent to parish children in kindergarten through third grade. Children in all the grades actually participated, however, sitting at tables according to grade. The twist to this particular celebration is that the youngsters themselves put on the party.

Everyone plays a part in its success. Throughout Advent, the children make plans and work on their specific contribution to the party: First graders make decorations for the walls, second graders make placemats and third graders make centerpieces for the table. Fourth graders color the invitations and fifth graders address all the envelopes. Sixth graders have the biggest job, planning the games and prizes. Seventh and eighth graders arrange the prayer service and work on the entertainment.

Thanks to the enthusiasm of creative teachers and volunteers, Advent has truly become a season of planning, preparing, waiting and hoping. During the Christmas break, the day for the party finally arrives. All the children are ready to celebrate. Each year we celebrate Christmas with the children this same way, with a few variations.

Always, at the end of the party there is a talk, ostensibly addressed to the little ones. But everyone listens. After a few years we became fairly sure that the older children, who had heard the talk several times by then, could give it themselves.

It goes something like this: We point out that while some people might be putting their trees out to the curb, we know that Christmas is not over yet. We ask the children if they know what we are celebrating. They all seem to know that it is Jesus' birthday. After talking about Jesus for a while, we remind them that one of the things that makes Jesus so special is that, even though he died on the cross many, many years ago, he is still alive today. We ask them if they know where Jesus is today. After the obvious answers of "in heaven" and "everywhere," some little child comes up with the answer we are looking for, "Jesus lives in us."

We explain how you can tell that Jesus is present when people love each other. Then we talk about the party and tell them what each class has given and shared. With that much love around, we say, we are sure that Jesus must be inside everyone at the party.

Happy Birthday

Finally, we tell them that Jesus' birthday is certainly something to celebrate, but that today we aren't just celebrating the special day that happened almost two thousand years ago. We are celebrating how that day has changed each one of us. Everything is different because Jesus was born and died and rose. His birthday is our birthday, too. We celebrate Jesus today, we say, but we also celebrate us. At this point we turn the lights out and bring in cupcakes, complete with candles to blow out. Everyone sings our special Happy Birthday song: "Happy Birthday to you. Happy Birthday to me. Happy Birthday to Jesus. Happy Birthday to us."

CHAPTER SIXTEEN

Living Lent

W orking for the Church is like working in retail. Not only do we keep evening and weekend hours, but we also find ourselves thinking about and preparing for the next season before we have had a chance to celebrate the present one. Once Advent wreaths are in place and choirs have started practicing for midnight Mass, for example, we sometimes find ourselves thinking about Ash Wednesday and Lenten purple.

Lent offers parishes the optimal opportunity for accomplishing the definitive aim of catechesis, "to put people not only in touch, but in communion and intimacy, with Jesus Christ" (*CT* 5; cf. *GDC* #80). If we take our cue from the Rite of Christian Initiation of Adults and see these forty days as a time for purification and enlightenment, we know that careful planning can help the whole parish, as well as individual parishioners, to grow closer to accomplishing that aim. As with so many endeavors the secret to success is to start planning early and involve as many people as possible in the planning. Encourage the planning team to be creative in choosing a variety of approaches, considering small- and large-group activities as well as intergenerational gatherings. I make several suggestions for parishes below.

Small-Group Gatherings

One of the recruiting points of Lent for small groups is that participants know they are only committing themselves to a set period of time. Our hope may be that the six-week experience will be so positive that participants will want to continue, but many group members sign on precisely because they saw five or six weeks as "doable."

Groups could be formed according to neighborhoods or convenient meeting times, gathering in homes or at the parish. Small groups could meet to discuss and reflect on a number of topics, using a variety of resources such as videos, books, short articles or lectionary-based Lenten booklets designed specifically for parish small groups (such as the Lenten reflection booklets published jointly by St. Anthony Messenger Press and the National Pastoral Life Center).

You might consider designing your own parish program. Since Vatican II, Lent has been considered an appropriate time to recall our own Baptism and help others prepare for the sacrament. Parishes might form small groups that focus on the baptismal rite. Designing a six-week process centered around the baptismal rite would offer members of your planning group their own catechetical opportunity to learn more about the sacrament and how it relates to their personal faith life.

To get them started, consider the following ideas. Participants in the first session might begin by talking about their own experiences celebrating the sacrament. They might continue by looking at the Rite of Baptism for infants, considering the question parents are asked at the beginning of the ritual: What do you ask of God's Church for your child? Participants might try rewording the question and answering it for themselves. Think of what an interesting discussion could ensue if already baptized adults were given a chance to answer the question, What do you ask (expect) of God's Church? The follow-up question, Remembering that we are Church, how can we make what we have just asked for a reality? could provide an equally interesting reflection.

Subsequent sessions could focus on the baptismal promises or some of the prayers or readings from the baptismal rite celebrated at the Vigil Mass. The Rite of Enrollment and the Scrutinies might also be discussed at the appropriate times. Planners would need to develop some suggested questions for reflection and discussion to help participants focus on their own lives, their own faith.

Small groups might also gather to discuss the Creed in the

weeks preceding the first Scrutiny and the Our Father in the following weeks. The elect along with their sponsors could be encouraged to join one of the groups. This allows more parishioners to become involved in the process and gives the elect an opportunity to get to know some new people. A special evening liturgy might be planned with all small-group members invited to be part of the Rite of Presentation of the Creed and the Our Father. Finally, during Holy Week the small groups could be encouraged to take part in the various ministries: doing the readings, preparing the environment or hosting a reception following the Easter Vigil.

Large-Group Suggestions

Small groups are not for everyone. That means parishes need to plan a variety of approaches for diverse congregations. Parish missions, bread and soup suppers, evenings of prayer, special devotions and weekend retreats are only a few you might consider in addition to whatever program or process the parish is using for small groups.

Parish missions. Since weeklong (or shorter) missions are always popular during Lent, you may want to engage a dynamic preacher whose ministry is retreat and mission work or look around the diocese to find a priest or layperson with a gift for preaching. Sometimes it is advantageous to have more than one presenter.

Choosing a theme for your mission can offer another opportunity for Lenten catechesis. Invite a few parishioners to begin gathering at the beginning of the year to discuss Lent—its rites and symbols, what it means or has meant in their lives. They might also read and reflect on the Sunday readings. Their objective would be to develop an overall theme with specific topics for each evening.

Bread and soup suppers. These sparse Lenten meals have been popular in many parishes for a long time, whether a one-night or a weekly event. Friday evenings seem to be particularly appealing. In my home parish the small faith communities have volunteered to prepare the meals, which might be followed by a guest speaker, Stations of the Cross or a prayer service. Donations are accepted to cover the cost of the meal, with the extra money going to outreach projects.

Weekend retreats. For years my home parish has offered overnight retreats for men and women. These valuable getaway weekends provide time for quiet reflection as well as wonderful opportunities for fellowship. Some of the regulars have made the annual retreat for over a dozen years, while each year newcomers add themselves to the ranks. Always, the elect and their parish sponsors are encouraged to attend, offering them yet another chance to meet more parishioners.

Intergenerational Gatherings

By this time you have probably gathered that I am a big advocate for intergenerational get-togethers. I believe such gatherings offer the most natural way for youngsters to learn and provide an excellent format for their elders as well. The gatherings can be family-focused, as long as all parishioners— seniors, singles and couples without children—are invited and encouraged to participate and activities are geared accordingly.

A Lenten family rally. Those of us involved in catechesis need to keep reminding ourselves that people learn through *all of the senses*. The way our churches look, smell and sound may teach more about Lent than a three-hour lecture on the subject. Often praying together and celebrating ritual as a community can help us to come to "know" our God in a way that no book or teacher could accomplish.

We also need to encourage our families to be just as intentional in creating a Lenten atmosphere and establishing special prayers and rituals *at home*. One way is to gather families the week before Lent begins for a Lenten rally. After eating together and sharing a few fun activities, spend some time suggesting a variety of things they might do "as a family" to bring Lent home. *Kitchen Table Gospel*, a catechetical program published by Benziger, is a great resource not only for Lenten family rallies but also for family rallies throughout the liturgical year.

Lenten wreaths. One of my favorite family Lenten activities is an adaptation of a family ritual that began years ago in my own home. When our children were young, they enjoyed the Advent wreath so much we decided to make a Lenten wreath during that special season. We made a wreath of thorns from the branches of the blackberry bush. We set the wreath on two squares of purple felt arranged to form a star. In the center we put a large column candle and scattered jellybeans inside the wreath. After dinner each child could take a jellybean for every good deed done, extra prayer said or special "goody" they had done without that day.

When the children became old enough to read, on Ash Wednesday we wrote on small rectangles of purple paper suggested good deeds, special prayers and sacrifices. Each of us could add six suggestions, two for each category. We folded the rectangles and marked them on the outside with a heart for good deeds, a pretzel to symbolize prayer and a cross for sacrifice. After dinner throughout Lent we took turns picking and reading our selections. The children could write whatever they wanted, but every year certain things always turned up: "Make Phillip's lunch for three days," "Take James's turn to do dishes" or "Give up chocolate for a week." Prayer requests, by contrast, tended to change from year to year, reflecting where we were as a family and what was happening in the world around us.

When I adapted this family ritual for our parish, it became a main activity for the pre-Lenten rally. A volunteer brought in the branches, freshly picked so they were still bendable. While the adults and older children formed the wreaths (using work gloves for protection), the younger children decorated the candles and felt squares with various Church symbols. Finally, the rectangles of purple paper were passed out and all family members took time to write their Lenten intentions. The rectangles were folded and taped, families with little children were given bags of jellybeans and the centerpieces were ready to be taken home to their own family tables.

At one church where I worked, the family group made a

Lenten wreath for the whole parish. Adults and children alike filled out dozens of purple rectangles. (They shared and mutually agreed upon ideas before they were written down.) Every Sunday, parishioners could pick another good deed, sacrifice or prayer intention for the week ahead.

Summing Up

For over a decade one of the focal points of parish Lenten activities has been the Rite of Christian Initiation for Adults. Occasionally it is important to remind our congregations what the process is all about and let them know that the *General Directory for Catechesis* suggests that the baptismal catechumenate is a model for catechesis in the Church (#90).

The catechetical programs we plan for adults and children, not only for Lent but throughout the year, involve more than teaching, lecturing and textbook instruction. Catechetical programming means process. If we use baptismal catechesis as the model, we must allow time for fellowship and storytelling, as well as handing on the tradition. We must incorporate symbols and ritual as we involve participants in all the aspects of Church. By using baptismal catechesis as our inspirational model, we find ourselves engaging in the two principal means of fulfilling the catechetical task: sharing the gospel message and experiencing Christian life (*GDC* #87).

It is important to include all of the types of approaches mentioned here in your Lenten planning. Remember to begin strategizing early and invite as many parishioners as possible to be a part of the process. The more people involved and the earlier you promote your activities, the more likely Lent will become a part of your parishioners' personal calendars.

Part Four
Those to Be Catechized

Introduction

> *To this end [growing progressively and patiently
> towards maturity, faithful and obedient to his
> word], as a creative and insightful teacher, God
> transforms events in the life of his people into
> lessons of wisdom...adapting himself to the diverse
> ages and life situations.*—GDC #139

W hat better way of helping people encounter God than by
following God's own approach? The *General Directory*
suggests that our own pedagogy of faith should be modeled
after God's pedagogy (see Part Three of the *GDC*). God's self-
revelation over the ages demonstrates great sensitivity to the
situations, limitations and circumstances of the chosen people.
Consider the ways in which Jesus drew others into closer intimacy. He was always faithful to the truth, but constantly adapted his approach as well as his words and stories to the people
he encountered. In other words, the pedagogy of God and the
pedagogy of Christ both accepted people where they were, and
built from there.

It is the same with parish catechesis. We have a responsibility to adapt catechesis to meet the diverse needs and circumstances of the community. We must take into account the
differences of culture, age and spiritual maturity (see *GDC*
#170), as well as the difference of physical or mental ability (see
GDC #189). In the chapters that follow we look at each of the
various age groups within a parish as well as those people with
physical or mental disabilities. The chapter "Catch-Up
Catechesis" deals with children who have received no previous

catechesis and are returning to the Church or asking for Baptism.

Like all of those whom we catechize, these young people need to learn about the faith by being incorporated into the faith life of the community. This is the way Jesus taught—by walking with his disciples, breaking bread with them, listening to their concerns and sharing God's own life with them.

CHAPTER SEVENTEEN

Facilitating Adult Catechesis

For the first years of writing the religious education column for *CHURCH* magazine, I kept telling myself that my *next* column would be about adult catechesis. Then when the time came to write, I would find some other topic. Next time, adult catechesis, I would tell myself, and proceed to write about Confirmation or preschoolers. I know I am not alone in my hesitancy to address the topic. Like other parish catechetical leaders, I have a hard time shifting gears. For well over a century, parish catechesis has been almost totally child-focused.

Yet for over thirty years every major catechetical document—from directories to papal encyclicals—has told us that adult catechesis should be our top priority. The most current document, the *General Directory*, says that adult catechesis must be considered the chief form of catechesis, and that all other forms should in some way be oriented to it (*GDC* #59). Still, in the vast majority of our parishes, neither catechetical budgets nor job descriptions reflect this vision.

Why? As catechetical leaders we know the documents are true. They make sense. We knew, even before the *Directory* told us, that catechesis should be about conversion. We know that discovering God's great love for us and growing in communion with Christ, the definitive aim of catechesis (*GDC* #80), is grown-up stuff. And we certainly know by now that if we are really concerned about helping children develop a long-lasting relationship with God, it is their parents we have to target. Yet year after year many of us still spend the vast majority of our time, and the parish's money, on instructing our youngsters.

Is it just a rut we are in, or is it frustration? Have we had too many experiences of introducing guest speakers to rooms filled with empty chairs? If it is frustration, perhaps we need to remind ourselves that adult catechesis is more than religious education. The lecture-style classroom model is only one limited approach to catechesis. Perhaps it is time to appreciate the other forms of adult catechesis that are taking place in parishes. Since adult catechesis is about faith formation, it encompasses a variety of approaches, such as missions and retreats, small faith communities, study groups, catechist training and other workshops. These are only a few.

If it is a rut we are in, perhaps now is the time for a new beginning—a good time to begin thinking beyond an instructional model of catechesis. Why not review and celebrate what you are *already doing* in adult catechesis and undertake some envisioning and planning for the future? Refocus the parish's and perhaps even your own images of adult catechesis. No big changes, just begin to plan for the new century of catechesis. What follows is a plan for a one-time focus meeting from which you may take suggestions to help you get started.

A One-Time Meeting

Gather some people by special invitation and general announcements for a one-time-only meeting. It helps if they know they are not making any long-term commitment and that all you are asking them to do is evaluate and brainstorm about the parish catechetical program.

Provide a comfortable environment, more living-room than meeting-room, if possible, and perhaps offer refreshments.

Begin with *their* experience. You might ask participants to think about a time, perhaps a significant moment or event, when they discovered something about themselves or their faith that brought them closer to God. After they have talked about the experience with one or two other people, ask them to share it with the larger group. It is a good idea to take notes on the various catechetical settings in which their experiences took place.

Connect their experience with Scripture and Church teaching on catechesis. Read the passage from Scripture in which

Jesus calls his disciples (see John 1:35-51). Remind them that Jesus is also calling them into an ever-deepening relationship. Tell them that the *General Directory* tells us "that the definitive aim of catechesis is to put people not only in touch, but in communion and intimacy, with Jesus Christ" (*CT* 5). Discuss the importance of adult catechesis. You might begin by quoting the *Directory* again concerning the primacy of adult education (see *GDC* #59). Ask participants if and why they think adult catechesis should be a primary concern of the parish. After some discussion, list on newsprint the various catechetical approaches (missions, retreats and so on).

If someone has not already talked about the process of the Rite of Christian Initiation of Adults, do so yourself. Mention that one of the reasons the Rite is such a positive faith experience for so many people is that it follows a set process. Let them know that the *General Directory* tells us that this catechumenate formation process should be *the model for all catechesis*. Make sure that they have at least a minimal awareness of the steps in the process.

The precatechumenate is a time of welcoming and fellowship, building a trusting atmosphere sharing our stories and introducing the Good News. During the second period, the catechumenate, we continue to evangelize, ritualize and share the stories and truths of our faith. The third period of purification and illumination is a time for reflection and prayer. Finally during the last period, *mystagogia*, we continue to celebrate community and sacraments as we discover deeper and deeper elements of our faith. This formational process is repeated over and over in one's life, as one grows closer to Jesus through the body of Christ, his Church.

Suggest additional catechetical possibilities. When we consider the catechumenate formation process as the model of all catechesis, we broaden our concept of catechesis to include many different experiences. Consider, for example, the following catechetical opportunities: prayer experiences, Scripture sharing, Sunday liturgies, opportunities of fellowship, service opportunities, religious education and intergenerational programming. (Add these to the newsprint list of catechetical approaches.) Use examples from your own parish to explain each heading. This is your opportunity to let those gathered help you highlight all that is going on in your parish.

Below are examples, gleaned from parishes, to stimulate your thinking:

Prayer experiences. "Prayer Nights" are scheduled evenings of prayer and fellowship (weekly or biweekly). Some parishes offer centering prayer, others a novena. Saturday morning men's prayer breakfasts are also popular in some parishes. The parish library, video or print, can provide resources for meditation or individual retreat days.

Scripture sharing. Small groups gather to break open the word, either the Sunday reading or a particular book of the Bible. Some of the groups are well established and have been meeting for years. Others sign on for just part of the liturgical year— Advent, for example, or Lent.

Sunday liturgy. This is our once-a-week opportunity to reach the greatest number of adults in the parish. Some parish staffs begin their weekly meetings by going over the next Sunday's readings and sharing their insights. Thus the pastor has the opportunity to bring a broader scope to the pulpit on Sunday. Successful parishes also focus on Sunday hospitality and church environment. Consider offering retreat days as well as ministry workshops for greeters, readers and distributors of Communion.

Fellowship. "The Gathering of Women," a group of stay-at-home moms, comes together on a regular basis. The parish pays for childcare. Sometimes the women discuss a topic or bring in a speaker; sometimes they just visit. "Couples' Night Out" is one way of giving married couples a quiet, candlelit dinner with tables for two or larger group settings. Sometimes the guest speaker suggests table topics for after-dinner conversation.

Service opportunities. While soup kitchens and thrift shops can offer adults the opportunity to find Christ in the larger community, parish-based service projects can also be catechetical experiences. Working together cleaning up the parish grounds or meeting on a regular basis to make items for a Christmas bazaar provide time for parishioners to get to know each other. These in-house work sessions also allow people informal theological reflection as they talk about their week and share their daily problems.

Religious education. Workshops, classes, lecture series and Scripture study are only a few of the ways parishes offer religious education or instruction for adults. Providing a lending library as well as a video library, using weekly bulletin inserts or making the diocesan newspaper available are all effective ways of helping adults catch up or stay current with Church and faith issues on their own.

Intergenerational catechesis. Some parishes offer intergenerational programming as their primary children's catechesis. Other parishes offer programming for sacramental preparation or as supplementary on a seasonal or monthly basis.

Soliciting Participant Input

Display the newsprint list of all the catechetical approaches mentioned. Ask participants to reflect on the faith experience they talked about at the beginning of the meeting. Ask them to identify the approaches that facilitated their particular catechetical moment. If they mention any not yet listed, add these.

Next, ask participants to brainstorm all the different adult groups within the parish: singles, senior citizens, new parents and so on. Ask them to help you identify two or three *groups* from the list that the parish ought to target for adult catechesis in the future. On a separate sheet of newsprint, brainstorm *issues* that might be of particular interest. Tape both sheets of newsprint to the wall.

Invite the group to divide into pairs to create some new adult catechetical opportunities for your parish. Let the group know that it can design simple one-time programs or ongoing multifaceted processes. Finally, before adjourning, ask participants to help you identify parishioners in the adult groups that were targeted who are particularly creative or are good organizers. Ask them to think of people who might be willing to come together for more detailed future planning. Mention that they are welcome to put their own names on the list no matter what adult group they belong to. End with a prayer and a big thank you. (This one-time meeting will itself serve as a catechetical experience for many who attend.)

Summing Up

In the past, thinking about and planning adult catechesis was sometimes a frustrating endeavor, a task we were prone to put off until next year. Catechetical leaders tend to focus on tangible events that are simpler to evaluate or on familiar tasks with happy, first-Communion-like endings. Truth is, however, that at times, we have to get out of our rut and take some risks. Going out on a limb may help us discover the forest right there in the trees.

Without naming it as such, most parishes are already approaching adult catechesis in a variety of ways. By gathering a group of willing parishioners to help you focus on what is *already* taking place, you have an opportunity to celebrate your efforts. By soliciting their input for future projects, you can become more deliberate in planning additional opportunities for adult catechesis.

CHAPTER EIGHTEEN

Youth Ministry:
A Renewed Vision

My husband and I first became involved in youth ministry when he was teaching a high school sophomore religion class and he decided to take the group on a weekend retreat. One of the young men volunteered his family's cottage and, sight unseen, a dozen teenagers and two naive adults set out for the woods. We ended up spending three days and two nights in a rustic A-frame. The boys shared the loft with mice and squirrels, and the girls learned to get through a weekend without curling irons and hair dryers.

Two Invaluable Discoveries

I had just begun my master's work in theology and was eager to convert anyone who would listen. Imagine my excitement at having a whole weekend with a captive audience! My enthusiasm lasted until Friday night when one of the young people straightened me out. I remember the moment well. I was pontificating about the heart of the Gospel message (Matthew 5:38-42) about turning the other cheek, offering your tunic and walking that extra mile. One young lady, Rena, jumped up from where she sat and pointed out how ridiculous this would be in real life. If anybody tried these things at her high school, she said, they would end up being laughed at and walked over. The rest of the group vehemently agreed. I was so embarrassed that I kept quiet the rest of the weekend. Letting my husband run the retreat he had planned, I played "mother," helping the kids with the cooking and cleaning up. It was a wise move. At the closing prayer service, Rena gave me a hug and said I wasn't as bad as she thought I might be at first.

Later that year the parish youth minister left, and the youngsters in that sophomore class asked if we would take over the ministry. Roger and I agreed, and began with a group of teens who met in our home and planned the monthly gatherings. We sponsored canoe trips and dances, hayrides and camping trips. The core group also helped plan and facilitate service projects, liturgies, prayer services and retreats. The youth group also visited the elderly, helped shut-ins and supported a third-world foster child for years.

Probably our favorite get-together took place each Holy Saturday, when the teens decorated the altar, proclaimed one of the readings at the vigil and afterward hosted an "Alleluia" party for the whole parish. The youth group spent the day together, decorating the parish hall, cooking and baking, and practicing their parts for the evening liturgy.

When that first sophomore class was ready to graduate, we all met one last time to plan the liturgy for their final meeting. They all sat around on the floor of our living room searching the Bible for just the right Scriptures to read. Suddenly Rena shouted that she had found it. "This is it," she said, "this is what Jesus is all about." And she proceeded to read Matthew 5:38-42, having forgotten our confrontation two and a half years earlier. The words seemed new to her now, her own discovery.

I learned an important lesson that night, too. You cannot "preach" someone into believing. The Good News of those particular Scriptures had meaning and validity for Rena because now she had lived them and experienced them in the Christian community of her family, her peers and her parish. The youth minister who preceded us had done an excellent job of helping the young people of the parish to discover the value of a faith community. Later, working with the parish's associate priest, along with at least a dozen other adult volunteers, my husband and I were able to extend that invitation to more and more youngsters.

The Bishops' Renewed Vision Statement

I was reminded of these early years by the publication in 1996 by the National Conference of Catholic Bishops of *Renewing the Vision: A Framework for Catholic Youth*. Using the 1976 bishops' document, *A Vision of Youth Ministry* as its foundation, this newer statement offers a blueprint for youth ministry for the new millennium. While the 1976 document reflected the style of ministry of which my husband and I were a part, the newer document recognizes that both society and young people have changed. It uses new research and our ever-developing sense of ministry to address the opportunities and challenges that face today's young people. It places a much stronger emphasis on integrating young people into the life of the parish, and engaging the whole faith community in a comprehensive ministry with younger and older adolescents. The renewed vision takes the 1976 document and expands it "to address the call to personal discipleship, evangelization, and leadership."

Three Goals

The original document offered two goals for ministering with youth: (1) "to foster the total personal and spiritual growth of each young person," and (2) "to draw young people to responsible participation in the life, mission and work of the faith community." The renewed vision adds a third goal: "to empower young people to live as disciples of Jesus Christ in our world today." All three goals are interdependent and equally important. According to the newer document, they "express the church's focus for ministry with adolescents, while encouraging local creativity in developing the programs, activities, and strategies to reach these goals."

The document stresses repeatedly that youth ministry is the responsibility of the entire Church community. Its pages offer a comprehensive approach that provides a way of "integrating ministry with adolescents and their families into the total life and mission of the Church." Indeed, the phrase "it takes a whole church" is one of several themes discussed. Other themes fall under the consideration of a comprehensive ministry with adolescents that is developmentally appropriate, family friendly, intergenerational, multicultural and involves community-wide collaboration, effective leadership and flexible, adaptable programming.

Eight Components of Comprehensive Ministry

Finally, the document identifies and describes eight components of comprehensive ministry with adolescents. The same components were described in the 1976 document; however, the renewed vision expands and develops each. For example, it separates the ministry of "Word" into two distinct components (catechesis and evangelization) and expands worship to include prayer—private and communal. The eight ministries named are: advocacy, catechesis, community life, evangelization, justice and service, leadership development, pastoral care, and prayer and worship. The document offers these components as a "framework for the Catholic community to respond to the needs of young people and to involve young people in sharing their unique gifts with the larger community."

Each component is well defined, using several distinct dimensions or essential elements. Ministry of catechesis, for example, has eleven distinct features, presented below in a much abbreviated form as illustration. They explain that effective catechesis for young people

— uses developmentally appropriate content and process

— teaches the core content of the Catholic faith

— integrates knowledge of faith with practical skills for living out that faith

— promotes a shared dialogue between the life-experience of the adolescent and the wisdom of the Catholic faith

— incorporates a variety of learning methods and activities

— fosters an environment of warmth, trust, acceptance and care, allowing freedom for young people to search and question

— helps young people apply their faith as they make decisions and face obstacles

— promotes family development by providing parent-education programs as well as parent, adolescent and intergenerational catechetical programming

— recognizes and celebrates multicultural diversity

— incorporates a variety of programming approaches, including parish or school, small-group and home-based mentoring, independent or self-directed programs, resources and activities

— explicitly invites teens to explore their call to ministry and the gift of total self for the sake of the kingdom.

Growing in Faith

Under the section on the ministry of catechesis, the document suggests a curriculum for both younger and older adolescents offering four faith themes for each age group: the profession of faith, the sacraments of faith, the life of faith and prayer in the life of faith. Each theme is more fully developed according to age level. As you probably have gathered, *Renewing the Vision: A Framework for Catholic Youth Ministry* is considerably longer and more detailed than its predecessor. This chapter can only touch the surface.

We did some great work in the seventies and eighties, and each year we learned more and more about effective youth ministry. This latest document offers a summary of that collective knowledge, providing sound theory and practical directives and suggesting further resources in studying the issue. It offers not only the framework, but also the blueprint for successful ministry with the next century's young people. For it to be most effective, however, it should be read, discussed, prayed over and implemented, not only by the parish youth minister and his team, but by the entire staff and probably a representative group of parish adults and youth.

Comprehensive ministry with adolescents, the document

states, involves the whole Church integrating young people into the faith life of the community. This is evangelization at its best. It nurtures young people as they grow, personally and spiritually. It encourages leadership through full participation in the mission and work of the Church and it challenges young people to answer God's call to be disciples of Christ.

Living Testimony

My husband and I continued to work with the youth group for five years after that memorable class of sophomores graduated. When it was time for us to leave, it was Rena who took over the leadership of the group. She was grown up, married and had a baby of her own. She and her husband volunteered their time and their home. Her parents, her peers and her parish taught her to say yes to the community's call. Today, Rena has three teenagers of her own. She remains a committed disciple of Christ, witnessing her faith at home, in her parish and in the world at large. Rena is a living witness to the power of a community committed to fostering the faith life of its young people.

CHAPTER NINETEEN

Evangelizing and Catechizing Our Children

V acation Bible School offers an excellent model for effective children's catechesis. In one short week, this summertime event can create a safe and welcoming environment for children, a comfortable atmosphere in which adults share the faith with them through personal stories and scriptural stories. Each day, the children walk away singing songs they have learned, retelling stories they have heard, and integrating the message into their lives. Vacation Bible School has always been one of my favorite projects, but only recently have I figured out why.

First, summer is a low-key time of year when the parish is particularly relaxed. No other groups are scheduled to use the classrooms and fewer parish meetings are held. The parish children can be placed at center stage. As a result those who come to Bible School may feel especially comfortable and welcome. Second, Vacation Bible School is rooted in realistic expectations. We teachers have only a week to ensure that the youngsters enjoy themselves while learning, so we focus on simple, fundamental themes, presented in child-pleasing ways, such as with crafts and music and games. Third, Vacation Bible School is a joy because the children themselves want to be there. They listen, they respond, they learn. Youngsters actually leave wanting more. By week's end both teachers and students feel the satisfaction of having accomplished something. What lessons can we draw from Vacation Bible School in order to serve children throughout the year?

Children Need to Be Welcomed

The parish needs to help its youngest parishioners feel as though they belong. Signs of welcome are readily apparent. When I was a young mother with four preschool children, for example, I could tell the moment we entered any home how welcome we were. I merely had to watch our hostess. It had nothing to do with what she said or did, it was all in the way she looked at the children. They knew it, too.

Parishes are the same way. Children can tell how welcome they are just by the way people look at them or don't look at them. The easiest way to evangelize children is by surrounding them with smiling, affirming faces in the classroom, the parish hall and church vestibule. On occasion, parishioners and staff members may need to be encouraged to attend to the parish children, acknowledging their presence in positive ways and expressing how important they are to the whole parish family.

Public rituals. Many parishes ritually "enroll" youngsters who are preparing to receive a first sacrament. In addition other rituals can also be planned for youngsters, celebrating the beginning and end of the school year with a special blessing ceremony, or recognizing birthdays at the end of Sunday liturgy. Rituals can be short and simple as long as they recognize young people and help them feel a special part of the community.

Liturgy of the Word. Many parishes regularly tailor the Sunday liturgy to children through a children's Liturgy of the Word, giving them an opportunity to understand and reflect on Scripture as it pertains to them and their peers. Leaders must ensure that such time with children remains "liturgy" as distinct from lesson-time or arts and crafts. Most such word liturgies are held in a room or building separate from the main assembly at Mass. When the youngsters join the larger community to hear the proclamation of the Gospel, the parish could, at least on occasion, publicly recognize them.

Some homilists also make it a point two or three times each year to preach to the children rather than the adults. One priest

I know of does both. Once a month, he calls the parish children up front and speaks to them for a few minutes before addressing the adults. It only seems fair, after all, since most of the time we ask children to listen to adult sermons. Some adults have said the most effective homilies they ever heard were those intended for children.

Comfortable space. On entering some homes, a parent knows instantly to advise the children, "Stay close and don't touch anything, we won't be staying here long." Some parishes, unfortunately, send out the same message, "Don't touch."

All children must be taught to respect property and possessions. They must also learn where in the parish plant they can run, jump and crawl without hurting themselves or anything else. Ideally there should be some space designed with children specifically in mind. Common areas in the parish ought to be designed to accommodate youngsters as well as adults. Our churches and their surrounding areas would then feel less like showcases than homes. Parish children need to be seen and heard.

Have Fun and Be Realistic

No one expects Little Leaguers to throw an eighty-mile-an-hour fastball, or fourth graders to master algebra—such abilities develop gradually. So it is with a child's religious development. The best teachers can do is to help each child experience God and learn about God (the Church and the world) as only a child can. Teachers must create for them an environment in which their faith can be ignited and the flame of faith can grow stronger.

Learning the faith can be a positive experience for young people. Why not offer weekend or evening programs celebrating the liturgical season (Advent, Christmas or Easter), or a Christian theme with activities that are enjoyable? (The activity, Sharing the Bounty, mentioned in Chapter Eight, "The Catechesis of Christian Service," on page 55, is one example.) Children's work is their play. Why not use it? Through creative games and interesting activities, young people will learn.

Youth ministers learned long ago that to help teenagers move closer to God and to their faith, they had to begin with them "as they were," ministering to their social, emotional and spiritual needs. The same approach works with their younger brothers and sisters as well.

Evangelization Works

Most of what has been said so far falls into the category of evangelization, that is, the soil preparation that precedes the harvest, when the Word of God takes root and grows. If parishes help their children feel welcomed and accepted, they are more likely to hear the Good News proclaimed in Sunday Scripture, discussed in religion class or explored through some special children's activity.

Of course, evangelization is most effective when the Good News is not only heard but seen. The most effective way a parish can evangelize its children is by demonstrating that it is a community of people who live daily by the values of the Gospels. The parish itself evangelizes.

The majority of the children in our parishes were baptized as infants in the faith of the community. The Church trusted not only the immediate family, but the larger "Church family" to witness, promote and encourage the faith life of those children. They were baptized not only in our faith but because of our faith. We have a responsibility to make that faith authentic and appealing—authentic by living the gospel and appealing by making Church a positive, affirming experience. In this way youngsters can grow up comfortable in asking their questions, allowing us to help them find answers within a faith they are willing to own.

Summing Up

Vacation Bible School demonstrates how to evangelize and catechize children. If parishes welcome and respect children, creating an atmosphere of trust, then children will listen. If religious educators and parents have reasonable expectations and provide creative learning situations that speak to the needs of children, then they will respond. If the Scriptures children hear preached are also demonstrated by those around them, there is a good chance children will begin to live the Good News themselves.

CHAPTER TWENTY

Preschool Catechesis

From our beginning, God invites us into a lifelong relationship. A newborn's cries and an infant's coos are responses to that invitation—in their first conscious moments children begin to reach out to the loving God who created them. With simple questions and idle wondering children begin the ongoing process of critically reflecting on their own life experiences. Why is grass green? Where do the stars go during the day?—these are faith-centered questions that begin a conversation that will, one hopes, continue for their whole lifetime.

The faith life of children is as vital to who they are at age two or four as it is at any other time in their lives. How that faith life is sustained and nurtured, however, is much dependent on outside influences, most of all on their parent(s). It is the family that lays the foundation and forms the infrastructure of a child's faith life. The parish has a responsibility to provide loving care and gentle catechesis to all of its preschoolers. We do this by providing nursery care for our infants and toddlers during weekend liturgies and by offering preschool programming. We have, however, an even more important role in sustaining and nurturing the faith life of the preschooler's parents, and offering practical help so that they can nurture the faith life of their child.

Loving Care and Gentle Catechesis

Parish-provided nursery care and preschool catechesis is not just baby-sitting time for parents who are at Mass. While this is certainly a great side benefit, it is not the primary reason for the parish to offer this service.

Nursery care. We have come a long way from the days when I would drop off my own children at the church nursery, taping their names on their backs and hoping they would share the secondhand toys they scurried off to play with. A few years ago I had the delightful experience of taking my two-year-old grandson to the nursery in his parish. On the walls were colorful pictures of Jesus, alongside photos of toddlers celebrating a Church feast day. There was a picture of my grandson with a wide grin in his face, holding up a sign that read, "Yea, Jesus!" Clearly more than baby-sitting was taking place here!

Since the nursery is the infant's or toddler's first experience of Church, try to ensure that it offers a welcoming, affirming environment consistently. Staff can be volunteer parents or teenagers, but schedule their shifts so that at least two or three people are present at all times, even when there are few infants and toddlers. If at all possible, try to have one person be a regular—present every week. This could be an early childhood coordinator or an extremely generous volunteer. Seeing the same face, even for a short time each Sunday, offers young children a sense of continuity and security. Remember, whatever face the children look into, whether paid staff or volunteer, they should be able to see reflected there God's love and concern for them. That is the most important gift the nursery can offer.

The room, of course, needs to be child-safe (electric receptacles covered, cabinet doors latched shut, no dangerous objects within reach) and child-oriented, with tot-sized tables and chairs, age-appropriate toys, designated areas with safe space for crawlers. If possible, try to provide a quiet area for infants. While there should be ample time for free play, some time should also be spent on other activities such as listening, singing or dancing to Christian children's music and listening to stories, especially age-appropriate Bible stories. Lead a simple grace before snack time. Since children function best in regular routine, it is a good idea to establish a set ritual, encouraging all volunteers to follow it.

Gentle catechesis. Much of what is needed for the nursery also applies to preschool and kindergarten programs. From the moment youngsters walk onto church grounds, they should feel respected and welcomed. At an early age we can begin the critical process of making tiny individuals feel they belong, that Church is their home, the congregation their extended family.

In preschool programming, however, lesson plans take on importance and volunteers will need additional catechist training. It is presumed that age-appropriate materials will be used. Most major publishers offer excellent resources. However, there is always the concern that the most well-meaning volunteer will divert from the provided material into areas that are not appropriate for impressionable little ones. Therefore, catechist training is as essential as is proper direction and supervision.

If the parish can afford to hire a professional early childhood coordinator, it should certainly do so. If funds are limited, then the parish needs to identify someone with the necessary talent and time who can be trained for this crucial role. Remember the old adage, "As the twig is bent, so the tree shall grow"? The parish's responsibility to its youngest members is important. Having someone who is trained to facilitate and direct the nursery and preschool program, as well as to work with the parents in those early developmental years, is an investment in the future of our Church that no parish can afford to overlook. More important, our little ones deserve no less.

Ministering to Parents

As important as our responsibility is to preschoolers, even more important is our responsibility to their parents. If God is going to be a reality in the lives of our children, then they have to hear God-talk at home. If prayer is going to be part of our children's lives, they need to hear their parents pray. If the Church's sacraments and rituals are going to feel comfortable and be familiar to our children, youngsters need to experience rituals in their own homes. An essential part of every parish's catechetical program is supporting, affirming and challenging parents by providing time for them to meet and network (with the staff and with one another), and by offering practical take-home resources and information. This is true for parents of preschoolers, as well.

We need to keep in mind that most parents work hard to provide their children the best they can offer. Today often both parents work outside of the home, and in many cases we are ministering to single parents who are doing the best they can with a double load. Time is at a premium. Energy is limited. Keeping all of this in mind, how can we help them? How can we support the parents of preschoolers in the crucial role they play in the faith life of their youngsters?

Regular communications. Send home a letter at the beginning of the year. Make sure it is an affirming, positive note that lets parents know how essential they are to their child's faith development. Let them know of your willingness to be there for them. Inform them of what resources and programs the parish has available for their own interests, as well as those resources that might be of interest to them as parents.

Send home a regular newsletter. Let them know what is going on in the nursery or their child's preschool sessions. Suggest books, videos or television programs that offer wholesome entertainment or faith-oriented educational tools. Offer gift suggestions, puzzles, coloring books and bedroom decorations that help create for a child a Christian environment at home. Offer simple prayer services or rituals during the liturgical seasons. And always reinforce the idea that the parish is there to support the parents as they help their child grow in faith.

Parent meetings. Occasionally invite the parents to meet together, after Mass or for an early evening get-together, with child care provided. At the meetings, you might offer practical information on parenting skills, or facilitate a simple potluck. Pay attention to the liturgical seasons: The beginning of Advent or pre-Lent afford great opportunities to gather parents for food and fun. In the process of the gathering, suggest simple practical activities and rituals to help parents change the secularized emphasis at Christmas and Easter into the special holy days they are intended to be.

Baptismal preparation, too, can be more than a one-time

class. Try extending the occasion into two or more sessions. Again, consult any number of excellent resources available from a variety of publishers. During your last session, plan some reunions. Plan get-togethers every six months to mark the babies' progress. Bring in a guest speaker now and then. Keep things simple. Sometimes parishioners who have survived their own children's "terrible twos" themselves give the best witness talks. Give parents time to make connections with each other, encouraging them to set up play groups or baby-sitting co-ops. Young couples often live at a distance from their families and old friends; by offering parish get-togethers you are providing an opportunity for them to form their own small faith community.

Some parishes offer an even earlier opportunity for young married couples to gather: prenatal Baptism classes that are combined with Lamaze classes. One parish in Florida works with the local Lamaze chapter, offering the use of their parish facilities for classes. Notices are placed in the Sunday bulletin as well as in the parish newsletter inviting pregnant couples to become a part of the Lamaze class. The couples who gather form a unique community. While they are learning about and practicing for a safe delivery, they are also discovering the importance of their ministry as parents. For a half-hour before the birthing classes begin, expectant moms and dads learn about the faith they received at their own Baptism, the same gift of faith they will be asking for on behalf of their child.

During all of these gatherings and meetings it is important to allow time for parents to talk and minister to each other, asking each other questions and sharing their problems. In the course of such conversations they are bound to discover how much they are learning about God and their own faith through their children and through the difficult, yet infinitely rewarding role of parent.

Teachable Moments

When my youngest son was a toddler, I used to sit with him on my lap and play a word game the two of us had made up. It was a simple game called, "Who loves you?" I would ask him, "Who loves you?" and he would list friends and cousins, aunts and uncles. Then I would ask, "But who loves you even more?" He would name his brothers and sisters, grandmas and grandpas. Again I would ask, "But who loves you even more?" With a louder voice he would answer, "Mom and Dad love me." And then slowly I would ask, "But who loves you most of all, even more than aunts or uncles, sisters or brothers, grandmas and grandpas, even more than Mom and Dad?" The final answer always came with a wide grin. "God loves me!" he would say, and the game would end with a great big hug.

Two summers ago as we sat in my rocker, I played the same game with my almost three-year-old grandson. We had played it before and Jacob knew the answers. But this time after he gave the final answer, "God loves me," he stopped rocking, pushed himself forward, looked me in the eye, and asked, "Who is God?" What a wonderful, teachable moment. We sat back and rocked and talked and talked. I learned a lot about God that day from my oldest grandchild.

CHAPTER TWENTY-ONE

Catechesis for the Developmentally or Physically Challenged

M y first experience as a catechist took place in Milwaukee, Wisconsin, when I answered a request in our parish bulletin. The Christ Child Society (a national organization of women who volunteer their time and energy working with children) was looking for people to teach religion to "exceptional children." At that time the Christ Child Society facilitated and staffed religious education classes for developmentally disabled people in twenty-eight parishes in the archdiocese. They produced their own materials and trained the catechists. They encouraged volunteers to complete the necessary requirements for certification. I remember taking a series of classes from a woman whose profession was training Montessori teachers. When I look back at those early years I am amazed at how well defined and developed that ministry was. I learned to "teach" religion as a multisensory experiential process. I learned to keep things simple and basic. Most of all I learned how to adapt, adapt, adapt! Those four years of working with developmentally disabled children and adults were an extraordinary foundational experience for me. They helped shape my whole vision of catechesis.

Our approach today, when working with the physically or developmentally disabled, has not changed much, with one notable exception: Rather than organizing separate classes, parishes today are encouraged to use a more "inclusive approach," teaching the children with disabilities in the same classroom as the other children. I know from my own experience the benefits of this approach, which extend not only to young learners but to their catechists, classmates, parents and indeed the whole parish. I talked recently with a colleague about the advantages of such inclusive learning in a catechetical setting.

Kathleen Kammer is a director of religious education who has taken a special interest in working with children who have disabilities. Her interest began the first week she started as a DRE. A parent approached her, asking for help with her seventh grader who had special needs. Kammer gave the mother some material for home study, but promised that she would find a way to integrate her son into the parish program. That promise became a top priority. Later that year Kammer approached the Center for Ministry with Disabled People at the University of Dayton, as well as the Cincinnati Archdiocesan Religious Education Office and asked for help. By the end of the year the parish where Kammer worked had begun to integrate children with special needs. With the help of the Center for Ministry, she developed a successful process for "inclusive catechesis" that she has been sharing with other parishes across the country. It has three important elements: a working committee, prepared catechists and active networking.

A Working Committee

One of the first things Kammer has done in two of the parishes where she has worked is set up an inclusive education committee. The committee is made up of parents of children with disabilities and various parish professionals with special skills—occupational therapists, inclusive education teachers in public schools, school councilors and behavioral specialists. Kammer told me that she has no trouble finding these people. She simply put a few announcements in the parish bulletin and did some parish networking to discover the volunteers she needed.

Kammer assured committee members that after the initial

formation period, they would need to attend only four or five meetings a year. The committee meets with first-time catechists to answer questions and make suggestions. They also serve as resource persons to catechists and parents, listening to parents, offering advice and support. The generous gift of their time and expertise was seen as a true ministry to the parish.

Preparing Catechists and Aides

At the beginning of the year all catechists and aides are asked to attend training sessions. The sessions help them rethink their approach to lesson planning. Catechists are asked to use the manual that comes with their textbooks only as a reference and to design their own lesson plans instead. Catechists learn how to prepare lessons that are simple but concrete, multisensory and experiential:

- Divide the class time into ten-minute segments, with a change of pace or space to mark the segments.

- Avoid written activities and instead focus on a variety of other approaches, such as discussions, working in teams, listening and telling stories, role playing, working with visual graphics, listening to music or any of a variety of simple, tactile activities.

For some parishes these training sessions inaugurate a whole new approach to catechesis. Since all catechists and aides are asked to attend (not only those who will be involved in inclusive programming), in effect, the entire catechetical program's emphasis shifts from didactic methods to a more experiential approach.

Another goal for inclusive catechesis is to station an aide or co-teacher in every classroom. The aide or co-teacher's role is not to hover over the child with special needs, but to work with all the young people, keeping an eye on the disabled youngster(s) to discern the occasional opportunity when assistance might be needed. In an inclusive classroom all the young people are encouraged to work cooperatively, lending a hand to anyone who might need it. If a disabled child needs help, it is usually another classmate who steps in to assist.

Two additional suggestions: (1) As a general rule catechists would do well not to call on children to read, but to ask for volunteers; and (2) youngsters in grades four and under are ordinarily fine about accepting children in their classroom who have special needs. They seldom need any explanation. It is wise, however, to prepare young people in grades five and above before a youngster with disabilities is introduced into the classroom.

The DRE gives catechists a confidential notification form when a young person with disabilities is on their class roster. This form lets the catechist know the child's special needs and offers suggestions on how to work with the youngster, and includes the telephone number of the inclusive committee member who is their personal contact. Catechists are asked to keep the form and use the back of it to offer suggestions and activities they have found successful. This information is then passed on to the next year's catechist.

Active Networking

It is sometimes surprising to see the number of children who come for instruction once word is out that the parish is offering an inclusive program for children with disabilities. This gives you an additional opportunity to minister to the parents as well as to their youngsters by facilitating networking on a national, local and parochial level.

List in the parent handbook the names, addresses and phone numbers of local and national organizations that might assist parents of children with special needs. Consider including as well the names and professional skills of inclusive education committee members. Whether their child is sightless, developmentally disabled or has been diagnosed with Attention Deficit Disorder, parents welcome knowing that there are professionals in the parish willing to talk with them about their special needs. It is also a good idea to invite parents to an occasional inclusive education meeting. In this way you can help parents begin to network with each other. Parents can share information and offer mutual support when given the opportunity to meet with each other.

Networking within an inclusive education program does not only involve parents, however. Catechists and DREs also need information and support. Occasionally take the opportunity to gather the catechists who are directly involved in the inclusive education program. Give them a chance to compare notes, share ideas, and support and affirm each other in their ministry. Remind catechists there are people with the necessary know-how who are willing to help.

The DRE needs to network within her own circle of colleagues as well as in the larger community. Often a nearby college or university has willing volunteers looking for an opportunity to help out. For example, the national organization, Best Buddies Program, an outreach of the Kennedy Foundation, pairs college students with developmentally disabled people.

The success of Kammer's approach and its long-range benefits were reinforced for me as I sat with her in her office. As our conversation ended, a woman knocked on the door and entered the room all smiles. She was a member of the inclusive education committee and the mother of an eighteen-year-old who had been part of the inclusive religious education program at the parish since he was seven. She was dropping off some flyers for a new program she and some of the other parents were initiating with the help of the rest of the committee. The program, "CHEERS" (Church/Community Helping Each and Everyone Reach Success), is an evolving dream of the committees. "It's a sort of social club for adolescents and adults with developmental disabilities," she said. As she talked about the club, you could see her enthusiasm and excitement grow. She told me that the club offers supervised recreational and leisure services every Saturday and provides opportunities for community interaction and prayer as well as planned activities, sports and short day trips. The organizers have long-range goals such as finding employment and living arrangements for its members. It is doubtful that any of this would have developed without the inclusive education committee and its network of parents and professionals.

A Mission for All

Kathleen left me with this reminder: People with disabilities have a mission, too. Their helplessness is God's loudspeaker, calling for a generosity that might otherwise go untapped. They are a constant reminder that there are more precious things than material possessions, power and influence. People with disabilities recall us to the values of simplicity, affection and complete trust. In this way they serve as our teachers, catechists in our midst calling us to compassion, inclusiveness and growth.

CHAPTER TWENTY-TWO

Catch-Up Catechesis

E ach year more and more parents bring to our parishes children who have received no formal religious education. Sometimes the families are asking for Baptism, but often they are already baptized Catholics who are returning to the Church. What we teach and how we teach it can be critical to how successful we are in incorporating the family into the parish community.

This process of initiatory catechesis reminds me of a Bible School ritual I witnessed for over a dozen years. We ended Vacation Bible School with this ritual by inviting all children to sit on the floor in a large circle and asking them to roll a large ball of yarn in front of them, each child passing it to the person on the right. Every fourth or fifth youngster taped the yarn securely in front of him or her. When the yarn had been passed to each child, ending up where it began, a large circle would have formed in front of the gathered youngsters. The children were told that the yarn was special and that inside the circle they had created sacred space. Only holy, special things could be placed inside this sacred space. With much ceremony the oldest children in the group placed a cloth from the altar, a large candle and a Bible. Finally, the children were told there was one more holy, special thing that needed to be put inside the sacred space. Each of them would be invited to stand, take one step forward into the circle and sit down again. Our prayer service would continue with songs, Scripture readings and prayers.

The movement within this prayer ritual is like the process of welcoming a new person to church or welcoming back the already baptized. We invite them to step into the circle of the community, help them to feel comfortable and encourage them to pray with us and share their stories. As in the prayer ritual, our role as catechetical leaders is to highlight, with the help of the community, the sacred that is always with us. We are to help others discover that wherever they go, wherever they are, Christ is with them—Christ is in them.

The Aim of Catechesis

The definite aim of catechesis is to put people "not only in touch, but also in communion and intimacy, with Jesus Christ" (*CT 5*). Christian faith is about conversion, the decision to walk in Christ's footsteps (see *GDC*, #53). That initial step into the circle of community is only the first step in a lifelong journey of conversion. This ongoing conversion process involves the heart as well as the mind, which means that evangelization and catechesis must go hand in hand. They are important at every stage of faith and absolutely crucial in the initiatory stage. Using the *General Directory for Catechesis* as a resource, I would like to consider the who, where, what and how of this process.

The Who: Children, Adults and Other Parishioners

One way of catechizing children who have had no previous religious education is to tutor them in small homogenous groups. When I worked in a large suburban parish, I would usually organize two or three such classes a year. It was not until I moved into a small urban church, however, that I could appreciate another way of preparing such youngsters for the sacraments.

A grandmother with three grade-school-aged boys asked to become members of our parish. It was the sudden, unexpected death of her daughter and the responsibility of raising the three young boys that brought this woman back to the Church. She had received little religious training herself, and the boys had received none. There were no other children in our small parish with whom to team them, so I decided to work with the family myself.

Every two weeks I met with the grandmother and went

over the material she would present to her grandsons at home. At the same time the family was invited to join the small family group that met monthly after Sunday liturgy. Our home visits were an opportunity for the grandmother and me to become friends and for me to hear her story. The family gatherings helped this small, newly formed family to get to know other parents and children in the parish. The gatherings also allowed the parish families to renew their own faith as they witnessed the enthusiasm of the newcomers.

Through this experience I learned that there are three different groups of people who can be evangelized and catechized in "catch-up catechesis": the children themselves, their parents or guardians and the parish community. While the children are certainly a primary focus, the adults who bring them also deserve our attention.

Parents are important because of the crucial influence they exert in the faith lives of their children. They are also important in their own right because in bringing their children they are also presenting themselves. We need to pay attention to where these adults are in their own conversion process. In most situations some reason or event has brought the family to our doorstep. In effect we are offered a golden catechetical moment to touch the faith life of the parents who present their children to be catechized.

Finally, the parish itself is the learner. By welcoming and supporting the children and families who are involved in the initiatory process, the parish can learn more about itself, about its faith and, through the Rite of Christian Initiation, about its ritual. Often, individual parishioners revitalize their personal faith by observing the spirit of the young people and adults being catechized.

The Where: Home and Parish

The evangelization and catechesis of young people needs to take place both in the parish and at home. The home is the first and most sustained experience the child will have of Christian living. The *Directory* tells us the "childhood religious awakening which takes place in the family is irreplaceable.... Indeed 'family catechesis precedes...accompanies and enriches all forms of catechesis'..." (*GDC* #226).

Unfortunately, many adults are uncomfortable talking about their faith with their children. Rather than confront parents, catechists need to affirm and support them by offering them resources to use at home and creating opportunities for them to network with other caregivers and families.

Initiatory catechesis also needs to take place in the parish. The parish needs to offer a systematic and comprehensive program or process of catechesis for young people (see *GDC* #67), especially children who are new to our faith. We must recognize, however, that the most important catechesis the parish offers does not occur in a classroom, but in the parish itself (see *GDC* #257). If we hope to incorporate youngsters into our faith community, we need to help them feel welcome, knowing that they belong. Children and their families need to experience the Church as their home. They need to be included in every aspect of parish life.

Earlier chapters discuss how parish and parents can evangelize and catechize young people. In quick summary, there are at least three ways to accomplish this: (1) Provide a welcoming environment, including youngsters in every aspect—liturgical, social and service—of parish life; (2) recognize the importance of ritual and tradition in the life of a child; and (3) offer personal and corporate witness to the gospel message. The same three ways are important in the home: providing a Christian environment, establishing family rituals and traditions and giving personal witness to one's faith in word and action. As the *Directory* states, "In a certain sense nothing replaces family catechesis for its positive receptive environment, for the example of the adults, and for its first explicit experience and practice of the faith" (*GDC* #178).

The What: Apprenticeship of Christian Life

So what do they need to learn? What are we responsible for teaching them? It is important to remember that while the parents and young people have taken the first steps toward full communion with the Church, they are still in the initiatory stages of conversion. The *General Directory* is quite clear concerning the fundamental characteristics of initiatory catechesis. It is a "basic and essential formation centered on what constitutes the nucleus of Christian experience, the most fundamental certainties of the faith and the most essential evangelical values." It is much more than mere instruction. It is "an apprenticeship of the entire Christian life" (*GDC* #67).

Remembering that our primary concern is conversion, we must concentrate on providing opportunities for both children and parents to experience what it means to be a Christian, specifically Catholic Christians. As Catholics, how do we pray? How do we celebrate? How do we relate and interact with each other, as well as with the larger secular community?

We also have a responsibility to share with them our most basic beliefs. They need to hear the stories of our faith and understand the words that express who we are and explain what we are about. They should be invited to share their own stories and encouraged to live the gospel. We need to remember, however, to keep it all simple, basic, fundamental. There is time later for continuing and "perfective catechesis" (*GDC* #69).

The How: Regular Family Programs

I think one of the most effective ways of accomplishing all this is by offering regular family programming, perhaps monthly, bimonthly or seasonal. Families should be encouraged to make a commitment to attend regularly so that the bonds of fellowship can be made and strengthened. It is much easier to orchestrate the various aspects of initiatory catechesis in small church family group settings.

God Is Calling, the family series I co-authored with Mary Cummins Wlodarski (published by St. Anthony Messenger Press), was designed with such family groups in mind. The process works best when the families have been a part of the group throughout the year. Yet even if it were to be used only during Lent, families of the elect would be introduced to a larger family circle, allowing parents and children to get to know their peers in the parish. The *God Is Calling* series offers family retreat days, a family penitential rite and materials to use when presenting the Creed and the Our Father.

These parish family gatherings can also provide the representative parish body suggested in the Rite of Christian Initiation for Adults for celebrating the rites with children. An ongoing group of parishioners who make up parish-based or neighborhood family clusters provides an ideal program of comprehensive and systematic catechesis for catch-up families.

Summing Up

A few years ago I took my ball of yarn to Florida with me where I was giving a talk to a group of parents. Afterward the children were going to join us for prayer. Just before the youngsters returned, we asked the parents to move their chairs to the perimeter of the large hall. When the children entered, we invited them to sit in a circle in the cleared area on the floor. We turned down the lights and I handed the ball of yarn to the child closest to me. The ritual began. This time, when the children were inside the circle, I said I wanted to tell them a story, so they all moved to the center to listen. After we finished the story and said a brief prayer, I asked them all to quietly find the eighth graders who had a "secret" they would share. (The older children had been briefed to tell the youngsters to bring their parents into the circle.) What a sight to watch! All those young people taking the hands of their parents and bringing them back to the center. When everyone was in the circle, we said an Our Father and exchanged a sign of peace.

I looked around as the youngsters and parents hugged each other and reached out to the other children and adults around them. I was reminded that, while the parent first brings the child to the Church to learn about the faith, it is often the child who ends up bringing the parent to the faith and the community that is Church.

Part Five
Catechesis:
A Shared Ministry

Introduction

Christ provides for our growth: to make us grow towards him, our head, he provides in his Body, the Church, the gifts and assistance by which we help one another along the way of salvation.—CCC #794

"Burnout" is a term familiar to every profession, and parish ministry is no exception. In fact, catechetical leaders are sometimes the most susceptible. We are a responsible people with job descriptions that keep expanding. We often find ourselves doing everything from making the coffee before meetings, to organizing a weeklong parish mission. As a result, we sometimes end up feeling exhausted, resentful and burned out. While Chapter Twenty-three, "The Catechetical Leader: Professional or Minister?," talks about the need for personal R&R (regrouping and re-energizing), Chapter Twenty-four, "Sharing the Workload," offers a possible solution for sharing the ministry.

If the words of the *Catechism of the Catholic Church* (cited above) are taken to heart, we realize we are not meant to do everything ourselves. People in the parish possess the gifts we need to share our ministry. Possibly one of the most important responsibilities of a parish staff is to help others recognize and develop their gifts and encourage them to use them. When this has happened, the job of the catechetical leader becomes much simpler. He becomes a facilitator, for example, helping parents or catechists find resources for sharing their faith with their children or working with other adults designing catechetical activities to enrich the whole parish. I believe the key is to call others forward, work with them until they feel competent, provide the necessary resources and then step aside and trust in the Spirit.

CHAPTER TWENTY-THREE

The Catechetical Leader: Professional or Minister?

In my early years as a director of religious education, colleagues were debating with strong feelings whether we were professional educators or ministers. Many felt the term *professional* was too remote and elite, while others thought the word *minister* did not convey the necessary academic background for the work. I have found that the most successful catechetical leaders are those who can be both professional and ministerial in their parish work. The problem is that the two roles seem paradoxical.

While ministry calls for personal involvement, the professional is someone set apart. Professionals have a special knowledge and expertise those around them do not have. For the director of religious education that competency crosses and combines several fields. We have advanced knowledge in theology or religious studies as well as some proficiency in educational methods, plus administrative and management skills. Our job involves designing, implementing and facilitating programs and processes that help people learn more about their religion and grow in personal faith and discipleship. We work for parishioners in a leadership capacity, which sets us apart.

On the other hand, a minister walks with the people, is a companion on the same road. In catechetical ministry we always minister *with*, never *to* the congregation. It is a subtle difference, but it is important. Ministering *to* people separates us. It suggests that we have something the others do not have, and of course when we are talking about faith, this is simply not true. Faith is a gift we share.

A parish catechetical leader's work involves more than programs and processes. The special knowledge and skills we have as professionals set us apart, but our faith as ministers binds us to others in the one body of Christ. Both are distinct roles calling for specific gifts and varied skills. Moreover, they probably attract different personality types. In the debate about being either a professional or a minister, many probably feel more comfortable wearing one hat than the other. Yet to be successful at our jobs we must wear both hats. Perhaps it is a good idea occasionally to take some time to adjust the headbands of one or the other. By learning new skills, fine-tuning others or spending time on retreat, we can make one hat or the other feel more comfortable.

So what hat fits you best? If you are not sure, just try listening to both terms: *professional* and *minister.* What thoughts cross your mind and how do you feel when you hear each word? Your immediate thoughts or feelings may help you instinctively to determine which role you prefer. Since your strengths probably lie in that area, you might consider focusing more time this summer working on the other, remembering that there is always the need for balance. Even those who already feel comfortable in both hats can use these two distinct roles to help determine in which area they need some regrouping and re-energizing (R&R).

R&R for the Professional

Summer is an excellent time to catch up on one's professional reading. A director of religious education I know saves articles from various professional publications throughout the year, files them according to topic and puts them away for summer reading. If you are not that ambitious, try keeping a collection of book reviews that interest you. During the spring reread them, selecting a book or two to read by fall.

A professional organization to which I belong sponsored a "July Day" for many years. At a spring meeting we chose a book to read, then set a date in July for a comfortable, informal gathering. We enjoyed getting together in midsummer for a leisurely day of good food, great company and interesting discussion of the book.

Summer is also a good time to investigate workshops or classes offered at local schools, colleges or seminaries. Or consider bringing in someone to offer a summer workshop for the whole parish. Gather a group of people who might be interested, find someone competent in the field to teach and set up times to learn together.

Would you like to find out more about Scripture or the new catechism? Do you need to fine-tune some administrative skills, such as time management or computer programming? Or perhaps the parish is planning a children's catechumenate for next year. Choose a subject that addresses the needs of the parish that might require your expertise in the months ahead, or just pick a subject because it interests you.

R&R for the Minister

Ministering with people requires a lot of energy and demands even more honesty. Sometimes it is difficult to appraise our own people skills. If you think this may be true in your case, ask friends to help you. Consider gathering a group of parishioners with whom you have worked and ask for their feedback. This gesture in itself models Christian ministry, since it allows the parishioners to minister with you. If you have specific areas to work on, check your local bookstore or library for material on skills development and techniques in dealing with people. If we are going to give our best in ministry, we need to do more than read books and develop new skills.

We need to take every opportunity to look at the source of our ministry: our own faith life. It is crucial to reflect on our own relationship with God. If possible, make time for a getaway retreat. Also set time aside regularly for meditation, spiritual reading and prayer. It is true that everything we do can be prayer, but I have to agree with the new catechism's assessment that "we cannot pray 'at all times' if we do not pray at specific times, consciously willing it" (CCC #2697).

Find a quiet place at work or at home, away from the

phones and out of everyone's sight. Pick a specific time—before lunch or first thing in the morning, for example. Give yourself an hour or a half-hour each day to reflect on Scripture or some other spiritual material, to talk with God or sit silently focusing on God's presence.

Summing Up

Remember, our primary job is to share faith, and we cannot share what we do not have. One's faith life does not remain stagnant: If it is not growing, it is diminishing. Sometimes we become so busy doing our job that we forget our goal. All of our educational, theological and managerial know-how and all the people skills we can develop cannot turn a person's heart. But what good is it to fill people's heads with religion and not touch their hearts?

The time we spend reading and reflecting, going away on retreats or for professional conferences and workshops is part of the religious educator's job. These are not things we do in our spare time. Many catechetical leaders have retreat time and professional days written into their contracts. If at all possible, parish money should be budgeted for both expenses. As professionals we need to keep current in theology and continue to hone managerial skills. As ministers we need to remember that everything we do, everything we are about, comes from and goes back to the source of all goodness and life. God is always with us, but we usually work better when we have taken time to be with God.

CHAPTER TWENTY-FOUR

A Pastoral Approach

A number of years ago, Dr. Françoise Darcy-Berube addressed a group of catechetical leaders, briefly outlining
what she called "a pastoral approach to catechesis." During the
talk she posed the following question: How can we make the
whole community more effectively responsible for the Christian
initiation and continuing education of all its members, both
young and old?

That question reminds us that catechesis is an ongoing, lifelong process in which the whole parish has a part. It is also a
challenging question to address as a parish.

One way of answering it is by making sure the question is
constantly being asked at the right times and in the right places.
In the pastoral approach described by Dr. Berube, catechesis
becomes the responsibility not only of religious educators but of
the whole community. It challenges all of the various ministries
within the parish to become more deliberate in their support of
the faith development of parishioners of every age. If a parish
were using the pastoral approach to catechesis, each member of
the staff would ask Dr. Berube's question, finding an answer
appropriate to their particular ministry (or ministries).

The question can also be addressed within catechetical circles. How can we, as catechetical leaders, help the whole parish
community become more effectively responsible for the initiation and continuing education of all its members, both young
and old?

Making People Aware

The most direct way of helping the parish become more responsible for its role in catechesis is to explain it to them as often as possible.

- When preparing parents for the Baptism of their child, ask them to think of their own response to the question from the Rite, "What do you ask of the church for this child?" Suggest they offer more than the one-word response, "Baptism." Ask them to face the congregation at the appropriate time during the celebration and direct their "considered" answer to the people in the pews.

- Before infant Baptisms, the presider can remind the congregation that the baby is being baptized in the faith of the community, trusting the community to witness to the child and to support the parents as they help the child's faith to grow.

- On Catechetical Sunday, include in the commissioning ceremonies some parish ministries not normally thought of as catechetical, for example, the liturgy or hospitality committees. As you commission each group, point out the catechetical role each plays. At the conclusion of the ceremony, ask the whole parish to stand in acceptance of their role as catechist, both as individuals and as a community.

- Challenge the parish staff to adapt Dr. Berube's pastoral approach for one week.

- Consider designing a one-day staff retreat to meet with an outside facilitator. During that time, look at each ministry's yearly calendar to see how it might address Dr. Berube's question, "How can we make the whole parish more responsible for the initiation and continuing education of all of its members, both old and young?"

- Choose an appropriate book or article concerned with the parish's role in catechesis to read and discuss with the education commission, parish council and parish staff. Dr. Berube's own book, *Religious Education at a Crossroads* (Paulist Press,

1996), is an excellent resource providing questions after each chapter for discussion.

- Make each parishioner aware of the responsibility each has to continue to grow in faith. Parish renewal, retreats, missions and small faith communities can help spark or stoke the faith life of adults, which naturally leads to a reaching out to others.

Sacraments of Initiation

The Rite of Christian Initiation of Adults sets a pattern of parish involvement that can be followed in all the other Sacraments of Initiation.

- Focus on the catechetical process, not on instructional classes.

- Develop a team approach, involving as many people as possible.

- Keep the parish aware of the process and aware of the people involved in first sacraments.

- Celebrate with the community.

This pattern can be adapted for Baptism, first Eucharist and Confirmation. With infant Baptisms, for example, consider sponsoring pre-Baptism sessions for parents that involve more than an explanation of the sacrament. Recruit other young couples to the parish at Sunday liturgy. Introduce the expectant couple to the parish at Sunday liturgy. And encourage the couple to celebrate the sacrament at a weekend liturgy or host a special reception occasionally to meet the newly baptized.

Continuing Education for All Ages

The best way to meet people's needs is to offer a variety of opportunities for all age groups. Ask for input from as many people as possible. It might be interesting to have the children do some planning for the parish, not just for themselves but for the adults as well. Ask catechists to brainstorm with their youngsters topics they think would be important for their parents and other parish grown-ups to learn more about. Let the adults see the list. Just reading the topics might be educational.

Another way of reaching both young and old is to include someone on the education commission or advisory team who will act as an advocate for each age group. Look for someone who would look at the programs sponsored for children and ask, how can this activity also teach the adults in the parish? Another person might have the responsibility of looking at the adult programs and asking, what are the children of the parish learning from this event?

One local parish asked that question last year while planning a weeklong mission. They had hired an excellent presenter for their adults and, rather than leave the children at home, they planned a program just for them. It followed the same nightly themes the adults were using. They recruited college students from the local university to work with the children and teens. It worked well. As a catechetical leader, look at the various programs for which you are responsible and ask yourself how they might be redesigned to answer Dr. Berube's question.

Teens and Elders: A Pastoral Approach

How might the whole parish become more responsible for the initiation and continuing education of all its members, both young and old? This was the question we tried to answer at the two parishes where I work when we were reshaping our Confirmation program. Both the liturgy and outreach committees were included in the planning as we worked together to design a process that would involve a cross section of the whole parish. We were also deliberate in planning a process that would build upon the gifts of our multicultural community.

It is part of the African-American culture to pay particular respect to community elders, honoring their wisdom and experience. For this reason we decided the elders should play a significant role in the preparation of our young people for Confirmation. The elders we asked were chosen because they were active and visible within the parish. It was evident that they were faith-filled Catholics. We chose approximately one elder for every two or three Confirmation candidates.

Preparation classes had begun the year before. The young people from three parishes met for a series of Saturday morning sessions. Since all three parishes are small and multicultural, we were interested in offering the young people an opportunity to meet other Catholic teenagers in the city. Confirmation was scheduled for the following November. The plan was that in the fall the youngsters would go back to their home parishes for the final preparation. It was for this final segment that we asked the help of the parish elders.

The week before the sessions began, the elders were called up to the sanctuary during the Sunday liturgy, blessed by the parish and charged with the responsibility of handing on the community's faith to this next generation. The candidates and their families were also blessed, and the congregation was reminded of its responsibility to be living witnesses of the gospel message. In this way we recognized that each individual, their families as well as the whole parish community, share the task of catechesis.

The teens and elders met together weekly for two hours on seven consecutive weeks. The original schedule called for forty-five minutes of small-group sharing, forty-five minutes of educational process and forty minutes of working together in some aspect of service. We soon learned that the schedule had to be altered because the small-group sharing took twice the allotted time. We ended up scheduling additional days to work on various outreach projects within the community.

The faith sharing made the program especially successful. The primary aim was to help the youngsters and elders get to know each other. They had been given the focus question early on so there were no surprises: They shared their life stories; the scariest thing that ever happened to them; the most famous person they had ever met. The elders were asked to talk about what it was like when they were teens, and the youngsters shared how they spent their weekends.

Both groups brought picture albums and their favorite music to share. They talked about themselves and about God and Church. On one of the last evenings, in discussing "the walking saints" in their lives, some of them mentioned each other.

Lessons in Faith

Confirmation took place at a Sunday liturgy, the young people from all three parishes participating. The commentator introduced the elders from each parish as well as the archbishop, the chief elder in our local Church. He then asked permission of the elders to begin the celebration. As the young people processed into the church, each was met by an elder of their parish who blessed them.

Both teens and elders learned much in those seven weeks, and the faith of the whole community was confirmed on that Sunday morning in November. That is the objective of a pastoral approach, by allowing the parish community to serve as catechist, each parish member both gives and receives lessons in faith.

CHAPTER TWENTY-FIVE

Sharing the Workload

Each year, it seems, the job of the director of religious education becomes more and more involved. No longer just "CCD principals," we continue developing programs outside the classroom to assist in the faith development of adults as well as children. Sometimes I think our greatest challenge is to provide both high quality religious education and to develop new pro- · grams without burning ourselves out. In a previous chapter I wrote about how important it is for DREs to reenergize and regroup. Taking time for rest and regrouping is essential if we hope to stay physically, spiritually and emotionally healthy. At the same time, it is also important to find practical ways of easing our ever-increasing workload. That is the point at issue in this chapter.

When I began working as a DRE many years ago, my job description was relatively simple. I was responsible for a weekly religious education program. I recruited volunteer catechists, trained them, scheduled classes and ordered supplies. I took care of sacramental preparation, summer Bible School and "helped out" with adult education. Ten years later, when I left my first parish, the job description had grown several pages longer. Included was responsibility for the Liturgy of the Word for children, a winter Bible School, separate monthly activities for youngsters in grade school, junior high and high school, an intergenerational family group that met monthly, as well as a group of stay-at-home-moms who met for support and networking. The parish had also added a video library and sponsored a parent group for fund-raising projects. We ran tutoring sessions for "catch-up kids" and were talking about beginning a children's catechumenate. I was also a part of the Christian initiation team and was responsible for the core team of small faith communities, training facilitators and recruiting new groups.

Struggling to juggle a full-time job with my primary vocation as wife and mother of five, I learned some valuable lessons during those first ten years. But it was the lessons I learned at home that helped me with my work in the parish. In both places, two issues emerged: determining ownership and sharing the workload.

Determining Ownership

I had the advantage of being able to stay home with my family until my youngest child entered grade school. During those years I did the laundry and ironing, the cooking and shopping, the cleaning and the picking up. I did not mind it. It was my job. Although the rest of the family shared various chores, the primary responsibility for the house rested with me. But once the children were older and I went to work, the situation had to be renegotiated. It was not an easy transition. My family was used to my taking care of them. It was not until I found myself near total burnout as wife, mother and DRE that the system was forced to change. And like any other system, the family system resists change.

The Church family is also a system that resists change in the same way. For hundreds of years, people in the pews had priests and religious to do everything for them. After all those years of being taken care of, it is no wonder that so many of the laity have difficulty taking ownership of the Church or Church programs. The parish priest is often aided today by a lay staff, but for the most part congregations still see their role as "helping out." As long as the parish staff is willing to keep running things, parishioners will see themselves as helpers.

That was the way it was at home, too. As tired as I was of "doing," it was still hard to relinquish responsibility or ownership. It was often easier to do a thing myself than to teach someone else to do it and then watch as it was done, never quite as well as I would have done it myself. What I learned from my children about helping other people take ownership is that I had to let go. If people value something enough and they feel fairly competent in what they are doing, they will usually do whatever it takes to get it. After I taught my sons how to use the washer, they began to do their own laundry, but only after they were convinced that I was not going to do it (and after the weather got cold enough they had to wear socks!).

By the spring of my fifth year in parish work, I felt the same sense of burnout I had felt as a working mom. So I decided to apply what I had learned at home with my parish family. I sent out an evaluation to all the parents and put together an evaluation for the children. They were asked to comment on all of the various religious education programs as well as the different elements within each program. I was fairly certain from listening to parents' comments throughout the year that the evaluations would be positive, and they were.

In May I asked the parents to attend a planning meeting for the next year. I told them that at the meeting we would be deciding which programs would be offered and which dropped. Almost half the parents who had children registered came to the meeting, which began with a discussion of the previous year's successes. Those of us leading the program read the results of the evaluations and thanked the parents for their support and help throughout the year. We explained that if the programs were to continue, we would need people to coordinate them, as well as work in them. We expressed our hope that we could discern those positions of responsibility that evening. We promised that the meeting would take no longer than an hour and a half, making clear that at the meeting's end, any activity without a coordinator would be dropped from the fall schedule.

We explained each of the coordinator's roles and pointed to the tables arranged around the perimeter of the room, each with a sign above it listing one of the jobs to be filled. People with experience in a particular activity were stationed near the corresponding table in order to answer any parent's questions. On each table were detailed job descriptions for a coordinator. Each job description ended with the same three items: (1) After six months, the coordinator would meet with the director to evaluate the job description, (2) the coordinator would hold the position for two years and (3) after two years, the coordinator would work with the director to recruit and train a successor. Parents were assured that each coordinator would meet regularly with the director and receive all the support needed. They were also encouraged to work in pairs—two people sharing the one role of coordinator.

We laid out the discernment process we would be using, then began with a prayer and Scripture reading. After a few moments for quiet reflection, we gave the parents fifteen minutes to talk among themselves, visit the tables and ask questions. Those interested in volunteering on a committee were asked to sign up at the table. Those interested in volunteering as coordinators were asked to sign one of the job descriptions and bring it to the director. Then we reassembled, announced the positions that had been filled and repeated the whole process: prayer, quiet reflection and table-hopping. By meeting's end, all positions had been filled. We had found coordinators for the children's Liturgy of the Word, children's activities, junior high activities, senior high activities, family intergenerational group, the mom's group and the parish video library. We also had separate coordinators for crafts, music and receptions and hospitality.

Sharing the Workload

Every year at the opening parent meetings, I would explain to parents how I saw my role as director of the parish religious education and faith formation. Like any professional, I would use my expertise to put together a program of action intended to bring about the desired outcome. Like other professionals, doctors or therapists, for example, I could only present programs of action for them to effectuate. I was willing to facilitate the action, but the parents themselves had to take responsibility and ownership for seeing that it happened.

If the desired outcome, for example, is a living and active faith life for children, I explained, then parents have to understand their part in the process:

- Parents must be committed to growing in their own faith life, giving witness to their faith, and consciously and verbally sharing that faith with their children.

- Parents need to understand the importance of praying with their children and attending Sunday Mass with them.

- Parents have a responsibility to urge their children to attend the various programs available for their age group at the parish and to support such programs by volunteering their time, talent, ideas and energy.

Before parents could register a child for our religious education program, they were required to fill out a volunteer form. Each year, as the program continued to grow, we added to the list of volunteer jobs. At one point there were nearly fifty different jobs listed for which a parent could sign up to offer help. Along with the usual appeal for catechists and classroom aides, we recruited volunteers to work with crafts, music and drama. We also encouraged parents to volunteer as substitute catechists and to help in the office. Adults presided at Liturgy of the Word for children, picked up audiovisual material at the archdiocesan media center and helped with the receptions following first sacraments. There were also at-home jobs for parents who had small children or found it difficult for some other reason to volunteer outside the home.

Examples of Volunteer Tasks

Calling substitutes. Catechists would call this volunteer if they were unable to teach. The volunteer would have a list of substitute catechists to call on.

Calling for audiovisual material. Catechists would call in their requests and let the volunteer know when the materials had to be picked up and returned to the regional office. The volunteer would have a list of people to call to do the picking up, delivering and returning.

Baby-sitting for catechists in their homes. Some volunteers would baby-sit at church, but stay-at-home moms and dads could also volunteer to watch children in their homes.

Sewing. Volunteers would sign up for simple straight-line hand- or machine-stitching for costumes, banners or craft projects.

Calling for baked goods. Volunteers would call people to provide refreshments for receptions, catechists' recognition dinners or class parties.

Always some parents and adults did not volunteer or would volunteer and then never follow through, but for the most part the workload really was shared. When the coordinators took ownership, my job became much easier. And although I left that large suburban parish a few years ago, most of the programs we implemented during my tenure continue. The director who followed me carries on with developing new programs and empowering parishioners to own them.

A workshop presenter once commented on the situation of a leader's leaving a job: "If people say, 'we do not know how we are going to function without you,' then you have not done your job." That is something to think about.

Summing Up

As a parish, we come together—with our children and neophytes—to celebrate, support, console, learn from each other and share all that we hold valuable. If parish is a family, then it should be a family of responsible adults who work interdependently to make all this happen. Pastors and parish staff must teach, nurture, affirm and challenge parishioners in their Christian responsibilities. Then, we need to step aside and allow those who are prepared to take ownership.

My children are all grown now, but we are

still family. We, too, come together to celebrate, console, affirm, challenge and share our lives with a new generation of little ones. Sometimes it is hard for my husband and me to realize that our children are adults. After years of taking care of and providing for them, it is difficult to wait to be asked for help. But I am sure that the more we respect them as adults within the family, the more likely they are to live as responsible adults in their everyday lives. Perhaps the same is true for parishioners.

CHAPTER TWENTY-SIX

The Parent's Role in Catechesis

I spent twenty-eight years in nonstop parenting and from experience I can say without reservation: The responsibility of sustaining, nurturing and educating another living person is a most difficult job. And I certainly believe parenting today is more difficult then it was when I began over three decades ago.

Because of today's culture, parents find it especially difficult to foster their children's faith and values. It wasn't always this way. Not long ago, virtually everyone believed in God and went to church, and the minority who did not kept it to themselves. The prevailing culture seemed to support basic Judeo-Christian values.

I grew up in a neighborhood where all of my friends—Jewish, Protestant and Catholic—learned the same Ten Commandments from rabbi or pastor, sister or priest. Movies we saw, records we bought, magazines and books we read supported our parents as they passed on to us the values that were passed on to them.

My parents also had the added support of a large extended family—a host of aunts, uncles and cousins nearby to support them. Our family may not have spent a lot of time talking about God or values, but there was no mistaking the fact that God was for real and, because of that, there was a code by which I was expected to live.

I grew up knowing I was Catholic, just as I knew I was Polish and American. My friends grew up knowing they were Jewish or Lutheran in the same way: It was an integral part of who we were. I went to the Catholic school and my friends went to CCD or to their own religious schools to find out what it meant to be Catholic, or Jewish, or Lutheran. When we went to our religion classes, the groundwork for learning had already been laid, and formal catechesis could build upon it.

For most children today, this is not so. Most parents have only themselves and the parish to rely on for support in passing on faith and values. Consequently, religious educators have to make sure that children possess the groundwork they need, lest religion classes become strictly academic. It is possible for children to learn the language of faith, without receiving the faith.

Often our first task is to convince parents of their essential role in the faith formation of their children. This responsibility goes beyond bringing their children to Mass on Sunday and dropping them off at religion classes or sending them to the Catholic school. We need to take every available opportunity not only to remind parents of their role but to offer support and resources for them to live it.

Parents' Meetings

The lives of child, parent and Church meet on at least three significant sacramental occasions: Baptism, first Eucharist and Confirmation. Most parishes offer—and many require—parent preparation meetings. It may also be helpful to require at least one parent meeting each year in addition to such preparation meetings, preferably in the fall.

The meeting content should involve more than the theology of the sacrament and the practical aspects of forms and instructions. Every opportunity should be taken to evangelize parents, helping them reflect on their own faith and encouraging them to share it with their children. Teachers must affirm parents, challenge them and offer practical ideas as to how they can work with their young people.

Affirming and Challenging

As a parent, I have sat through enough parent meetings to

know that I do not like being scolded or made to feel guilty about the way I am raising my child. As a working mother I did my best. And I have appreciated it when a teacher leading the parent meeting recognized that fact.

Parents need to be affirmed. They need recognition of the difficulties they face. We can help parents realize that simply by being good parents, they teach their child about God. When a child's "I'm sorry" is met with a smile and a hug, the youngster learns about reconciliation and forgiveness. Every time a crying infant is picked up and held closely, the child is learning to trust—an essential component in the development of faith. Parents who love and protect their child lay the groundwork for a strong faith life. Unfortunately, in today's culture that groundwork is no longer enough. Parents have to do more.

Parents and Their Child's Faith

Most parents, of course, want their children to have faith. They tell us this by coming to parent meetings and by sending their children to religious education programs or schools. The problem is that parents sometimes have the misconception that religious instruction can *give* faith to their child. After all, they reason, isn't that the way it worked for their parents and their parents' parents? It is up to the parish staff to correct such misunderstandings and, in the kindest of ways, challenge parents to rethink their role in their child's faith life. The parent's role is formative, it is primary.

A good way to begin a parent meeting is to ask parents why they have come. Why is it important to them that their child receive Baptism? Eucharist? Confirmation? Why have they enrolled their children in the Catholic school or in the religious education program? Direct parents to talk about these questions in small groups (or with the person beside them). Catechetical leaders must then listen to their answers, helping them probe deeper.

Share with parents a viewpoint such as the one expressed in the first few paragraphs of this article. Parents realize the world has changed; they know all the pressures facing their children.

After all, they face those same pressures. Point out that what may have worked before will not work today; if parents want their children to grow up believing in God and living their life in faith, they have to do more than their parents did and the parish also will have to do more. If parents and parish want their children to have faith, they will have to share their own faith with them.

Help parents understand that sharing one's own faith may not be easy. In fact, it may be uncomfortable, especially for parents who have been Catholic since infancy. Some people regard faith as a private, personal matter. It may be difficult for them to pray aloud or to read Scripture, even to their children. To talk about God might seem to be risky. Nevertheless, that is the challenge we must offer parents. It is the risk they must take. If they want their children to believe, then their children will have to see and hear that they believe. If parents want their children to pray, they will have to let their children see and hear them pray. If parents want their children to know about God, they will have to share stories about God with them—their own stories and stories from Scripture. This idea may be new for some parents.

Parish Suggestions

Here are some suggestions parishes and religious educators may take up to assist parents with "Godtalk" in their homes.

- Hold parish-sponsored family nights (or afternoons) during Advent or Lent. These provide an opportunity to bring families together to talk about how they can celebrate these seasons at home. Various published materials are available.

- Host a parish book fair. Arrange with a local religious goods store to sell books, videotapes and other religious items after all the Masses on a particular weekend. Make sure a wide selection of children's books for all ages and reading levels are included.

- Offer a media literacy workshop for parents. Contact your

diocesan offices to see what materials and resources they have to offer. In addition, you may want to invite someone who is knowledgeable to speak.

- Publish Scripture reflections in the bulletin. Include simple discussion questions, practical and life-centered, appropriate for children and adults. Address the Sunday readings in ways simple enough to be talked about in the car on the way home from Mass or around the dinner table.

- Subscribe to a children's Gospel weekly. Show parents how to use it and persuade them of the usefulness of taking time to do it.

- Use the family pages many textbooks offer. Find a way (other than through the child) to send books home, or at least alert parent(s) on what day to expect them.

- Suggest to parents that every home have a children's Bible and that parents read to their children from it.

- Discuss with parents the importance of family prayer, grace at meals, a blessing at dinner or before bed. Send home with children simple prayer services.

- Suggest to parents that there be some indications—a crucifix, a picture, a family Bible—somewhere in the house and in the child's room that says this is a Christian home.

- Help parents get to know one another and organize parent-support groups. Offer time and parish space for parents to come together to be with each other and share ideas and concerns.

Summing Up

We know parents have the primary role in the faith development of their children. No matter how much time and money parishes put into Catholic schools and religious education programs, the effects will be minimal in comparison to the influence the child's own home exerts. It would be to everyone's advantage, especially the child's, if parishes would start spending more time, energy and money on working with parents. We must take every opportunity to address parents' needs, helping them grow so strong in their own faith that their actions and words will speak to their children. This is one way of guaranteeing that the faith will be passed on to the next generation.

CHAPTER TWENTY-SEVEN

Faith:
It's All in the Family

A fter sixteen years as a director of religious education, I took the position of family faith minister at a midsized downtown parish. I had always appreciated the importance of family catechesis and included it in parish programming, but the process was always supplementary. At the downtown parish, family catechesis was the *only* formal children's catechesis offered, outside of sacramental preparation. At the end of my first year, I was more convinced than ever that family catechesis is one of the most effective ways of affecting the faith life of children and adults alike.

The first thing I did when I arrived was to call a meeting of the adults involved in the program. Not only young parents of school-age children came, but also parents with teens and children who were already grown. Each of them told me how important the program was not only for their children but for themselves as well. They spoke of how they had watched their children grow in their faith. They talked about how much they had learned in the process of teaching their own children. They told me how great it was not to have to force their kids to come to church. I had parents tell me that on some extra busy weekend when they suggested skipping a family meeting, it was their children who insisted they rearrange their schedule so that they would not miss the gathering.

It was obvious to me after this initial adult meeting that family catechesis was an important part of the life of each of the families involved. I was impressed with their enthusiasm, but because of my previous experience with parish-sponsored family programming, I was not surprised.

The family program met twice a month with follow-up reading and activities to do at home. But family catechesis can work in a variety of ways. It can be parish based and parish planned. It can also be less formal, centered in people's homes, around dinner tables or family room fireplaces. The important thing is that parishes begin to realize the shift in emphasis in children's catechesis.

At one time our efforts were geared to convince parents that they had to support what we were doing in our parish schools and religious education programs. Today that equation is reversed: Parishes have to do everything they can to support parents if we want children to grow in their faith.

Affirming and Supporting Parents as Teachers

So how do we begin to extend that support? Our first responsibility is to make sure we take every opportunity to affirm parents for the job they are *already* doing. We need to help them see that their everyday actions at home are laying the foundation for their child's faith system. Whenever parents comfort a child who is hurt, forgive or ask to be forgiven, give a hug for no reason at all or share that last chocolate-chip cookie, they help their child to trust, seek reconciliation and learn to be generous. They are teaching their child about faith, hope and love.

In addition to affirming parents, we need also to offer support. Today's parents have a difficult job. They are trying to raise children in a country that preaches individualism and in a culture where you can never have enough. The cost of living is staggering, the pace of life, frantic. Working parents, often separated from their extended families and isolated from their neighbors, may feel alone and frustrated in their efforts to teach their children values that conflict with the culture. Our job as parish is to help them connect with other parents and families so that they can begin to network and support each other.

Helping Parents Network

We can help parents meet other parents in many ways. Sacramental preparation meetings are a good way to begin networking. If we hope to help people to get to know each other, however, the meeting needs to address more than the who, what and when of the sacrament. Each session should begin with a discussion question. For example, asking parents of Confirmation candidates what they find most rewarding and challenging about living with a fourteen-year-old gives them a chance to commiserate and celebrate the experience of raising a young teenager. Parents of adult children can give wonderful witness talks, sharing their experiences and struggles, and testifying to the fact that there is a light at the end of the tunnel. In the process of learning more about their children, parents inevitably learn more about themselves.

Infant Baptism preparation can provide an opportunity for expectant parents to talk about their concerns and expectations. Try posing at the meeting the question they will be asked in the baptismal ritual, "What do you ask of the Church for your child?" Given enough time to reflect, their responses are usually more personal and profound than the one-word answers suggested in the book of rites.

Many parishes center sacramental preparation for first Eucharist and Reconciliation in the home. Parents prepare their own children, meeting occasionally with other families to get to know each other and to share what they have learned. Several publishers offer programs that are designed to fit this model.

Some parishes also sponsor regular get-togethers for parents: breakfasts for dads, afternoon or evening gatherings for moms. Sometimes outside speakers are brought in, or videotapes are used, but often the time is just spent with some prayer and a lot of talking and sharing. Time together for fellowship is always important, and offering baby-sitting is a big plus.

Occasional Family Gatherings

You can help to bring families together by sponsoring a few special events during the year. Picnics, prayer services, liturgies, service projects and even dances provide occasions for families to come together. They also make church feel like home.

One parish sponsors an annual "fifties" dance for families. All ages come dressed in appropriate garb: seven-year-olds with hair slicked back and teenagers in poodle skirts. There are hula hoop and limbo contests. Adults and children "stroll" and jitterbug together. Families sit at long tables with other families eating hot dogs and swapping stories. The next day at Mass people are likely to encounter a new acquaintance and see familiar faces from the night before. The dance is a regular event that adults and children alike look forward to each year.

One parish I worked at had an annual family retreat. About twenty families would take over a Girl Scout camp for a weekend. There was always prayer and quiet time, witness talks and small-group activities, but most memorable were the Saturday night festivities. I remember the skits the teenagers put on and the Family Olympics, with such challenging events as paddle ball, jump rope and jacks.

Many parishes schedule annual family rallies that celebrate the liturgical year. Advent, Christmas, Lent, Easter and Pentecost offer opportunities for families and other parishioners to come together to find out more about their faith, their Church and its special seasons. Making take-home materials available allows households to continue the celebration at home. With planning, your parish saint's day or feast day can become a time to gather families, celebrating and learning together. With a little effort and creativity, parishes can help build strong families by making sure some family time is a part of each year's parish schedule.

All of these suggestions are part of family catechesis. (Affirming and supporting parents has to be a major concern in our parishes.) Once parents feel accepted and supported we can take the next step of gently challenging them to become more deliberate in developing their own faith life and sharing their faith with their children. One way of helping them meet that challenge is to offer recurrent family programming, by which I mean facilitating family groups that meet regularly.

Regular Family Meetings

I facilitated a family group that met monthly at the first parish where I worked. The adults would meet at the end of May and set the agenda for the next year. The program was varied; if one month we did something educational, the next month our activity would be social. We had road rallies and scavenger hunts. We had guest speakers who helped us learn to communicate more effectively or negotiate household rules. We also studied Scripture and learned about the saints. In those days there were few available resources, so the adults researched and planned their own presentations, developing imaginative ways to reach even the youngest of our children.

Today there are a variety of family programs available (including the *God Is Calling* series) and planning is much easier. It is still a good idea, however, to involve as many adults as possible. Even the best resources are made better when adapted and enriched to meet the needs of a particular group. Gather a team of advisors to work with you, ask for volunteers to coordinate the various jobs. Two or three families can sign up to facilitate a particular month's activity or provide refreshments and hospitality. Working together gives people a chance to get to know each other, which is how we build community.

Sundays are usually a good time to meet. The gatherings can last one to three hours. During their time together, youngsters and adults interact, discuss and learn new things about their faith through a whole variety of activities. Table fellowship is also important. If you meet Sunday mornings, begin with doughnuts or bagels. If you meet in the afternoon, end with a potluck, pizza or some other simple meal.

Finally, because ritual is important in all families, including parish families, it is a good idea to follow the same format each time you meet. At the downtown parish we began each gathering by announcing birthdays and anniversaries and then sharing our own "good news," by catching up with all the "good stuff" that had happened since we last met. We had prayers of petitions and thanksgiving, a Scripture reading and then the planned session. We always ended with a closing prayer or ritual.

What Do You Learn in Family Catechesis?

Regular family programming can cover a variety of topics. While each published program offers its own scope and sequence, most programs cover the fundamental elements of the faith. At parish gatherings *and* at-home sessions, families learn about Scripture, the life of Jesus, Church life, the sacraments and how disciples of Jesus are called to live. Meanwhile, children and adults learn to become more comfortable talking about God and what they believe. Religion, prayer and ritual are not just something that happens at church. They begin to see their faith as an integral part of their everyday life. The *General Directory* tells us that the "religious awakening which takes place in the family is irreplaceable" (*GDC* #226). Regularly scheduled family programming helps parents become more intentional in helping that happen.

Important also is that the whole parish understand that family programming, regularly scheduled or occasional gatherings, is open to everyone. In flyers and announcements make sure you are clear that *everyone* is a part of the parish family: Grandparents, singles, couples without children are all members of the parish family and welcome at all "family" activities. The big plus with formal family programming is that you are building community. When people, children and adults (single or married, young or old), meet on a regular basis they get to know each other, trust each other and become "family." They learn to be Church together.

Summing Up

The *General Directory* recognizes the importance of family catechesis by telling us that family catechesis precedes, accompanies and enriches all other forms of catechesis (see *GDC* #226). I knew that even before the *Directory* was written, since my own family had been a part of a monthly family program for ten years. I know the advantages of such programming not only from the facilitator's point of view but also from the parent's. When children come back to our home parish for the holidays there is always a mini-family reunion as they reconnect with the other young adults they grew up with in that family group. The parents who were involved still get together once or twice a year for our own reunion. Over the years we have been through a lot together. We have celebrated weddings and buried spouses. Through those once-a-month meetings we became family to each other. And is that not one of the things Church is supposed to be about?

CHAPTER TWENTY-EIGHT

Preparing Catechists

D irectors of religious education have varying responsibilities: sacramental preparation, small faith communities, the Rite of Christian Initiation of Adults and family programming, to name only a few. Each fall, however, when school is about to begin, a director's attention is usually focused on gathering supplies, drawing up class lists and, most importantly, training catechists. Although working with catechists is a year-round endeavor, if one takes extra time at the beginning of the year to get things off to a good start, more than likely the whole year will run more smoothly.

Since Jesus was responsible for preparing the first catechists, he is a great model for those of us who are parish DREs. While we certainly have the responsibility to share the Good News ourselves, we have an even greater responsibility to prepare others to do it. Like Jesus who never left Palestine, we get to stay at home base while we invite, prepare and commission others to go out and share the word. It seems appropriate to spend a little time reflecting on why Jesus was so successful.

1. Jesus personally invited his disciples to follow him.

Broadly based requests for catechists, such as bulletin or pulpit announcements, often give the impression that any warm body will do. Experience has proven that when people are personally approached, they are more likely to consider the request seriously.

One way of recruiting new catechists is by asking a group of parents and parishioners to help you discern people for this ministry. Make sure the parish knows when and why you are meeting. Ask the parish for their prayers. Once you have gathered the group and spent time in prayer yourselves, discuss what qualities are needed in a catechist. Pray again, and then ask the group to go through the parish list, looking for names that "call out" to them. Take good notes on why they think certain people would make good catechists. If possible, invite those people yourself. Let them know what qualities the group is looking for and why members thought selected persons would make good catechists. Ask the invitees to pray about it. Tell them someone will be calling them back to receive their answer. Finally, ask the people in the discerning group to make the follow-up calls.

2. Jesus knew the people he gathered.

He knew who they were and where they worked. He knew their life stories. Get to know your parish catechists. Take time before or after classes to stop in and visit a few minutes. Plan in-service or retreat days and other opportunities to spend time together. If possible, start the year with a daylong orientation session. Begin on a Saturday morning, inviting new catechists for the day and asking returning catechists to join you for lunch and the afternoon. Spend time in large groups and small groups getting to know each other. A daylong orientation affords time for you to help the catechists feel comfortable and capable in their new role.

3. Jesus answered his disciples' questions and anticipated their needs.

Volunteer catechists usually feel more comfortable when they know exactly what is expected of them. Providing written job descriptions is one way of making sure catechists know their responsibilities. While religious education programs vary from parish to parish the list below gives an idea of what might be included.

Responsibilities of the catechist:

- Contact parents and children at the beginning of the year to introduce yourself.

- Prepare lessons and maintain discipline in the classroom.

- Arrive in the building fifteen minutes prior to class time.

- Take attendance.

- Fill out progress reports to parents at the appropriate time.

- Keep parents informed of what is being covered in class.

- Arrange for a substitute if unable to attend a class.

- Let the director know if your group will be meeting outside of your designated space.

- Keep the classroom in reasonably good order. Turn out lights, close windows when leaving.

- Attend catechists' meetings, unit grade level meetings and in-service days.

- Follow diocesan policies, and if at all possible, work toward diocesan certification.

First-time catechists also have questions concerning practical needs and basic housekeeping. What supplies does the parish provide? Where can they be found? If additional supplies are purchased, will the volunteer be reimbursed? What resources, such as televisions and VCRs, does the parish have available? How are these resources requested? What latitude do catechists have in setting up their classrooms? What about classroom snacks and parties? The list can go on indefinitely. One way of anticipating the needs of next year's catechists is by keeping track of the questions this year's catechists ask throughout the year. During the initial orientation meeting, make sure you present the job description and address all anticipated questions. Also build in time for the catechists to make other inquiries, in formal and informal settings.

Some DREs put together a parish handbook for catechists.

A simple folder with both loose-leaf binding and pockets serves well. Pages can be added throughout the year, and the pockets hold the booklets and brochures given out by the parish and diocese. Go through the handbook contents at the orientation meeting.

> *Suggested contents for catechist's handbook:*
> Calendar for the year
> Written job description
> List of important phone numbers
> Substitute teacher list
> Copy of student evaluation form
> List of parish resource material (games, videos, maps, etc.)
> Information on how to request and obtain diocesan
>   resources
> Copy of parish policies, (discipline, attendance, snow
>   days, etc.)
> Copy of diocesan policies
> Reprints of relevant articles, (i.e., class management,
>   designing prayer services, etc.)

4. Jesus taught with authority.

Let people know that you believe in what you are doing and stay abreast of what is happening in the world of theology and catechesis. Know your resources and share that information with the catechists. During orientation, allot a period for first-timers to review the materials. Spend time with catechists going through the books they will be using. Look at the basic format of each unit and point out how the catechetical process is incorporated into each lesson. Also, go through the catechists' guides, noting the sections before and after the lessons that offer valuable background on the subject matter as well as the age group with whom they are working. Go over the scope and sequence chart that most publishers provide. This will help the catechist see how the lessons they cover fit into the larger picture. Call their attention to parent pages or any other suggested means of involving parents the publishers offer. Explain any supplementary materials provided in the series and encourage browsing.

5. Jesus built community.

On orientation day, structure time, both morning and afternoon, for catechists to get to know each other and to network. Spending time together benefits both first-time and experienced catechists. Newcomers can receive useful, practical advice and link with valuable resource persons. Returning catechists find that their experience is valued. Ask returning catechists to share any successes from the previous year(s). Encourage newcomers to ask questions.

Larger parishes have the advantage of gathering catechists according to grade levels. You might give people a few questions or statements on which to reflect privately. Allow a few minutes for them to jot down their thoughts. Then open the period for group discussion. Below are some discussion starters that might help with grade-level gatherings.

Discussion starters:

Describe your age group of students.

What do you find challenging about this age group?

What do you most enjoy about this age group?

Discuss one lesson that worked really well.

Share a favorite prayer service.

What has been effective in helping your young people get to know you?

What has been effective in helping you to get to know your young people?

What outside resources (including people) have proved valuable?

What are you looking forward to most this year?

6. Jesus knew the importance of table fellowship.

Gather volunteers for formal Christmas dinners and casual family picnics. Send invitations and, once in a while, host a meal to which catechists need not bring anything. I learned this lesson early on as a volunteer catechist. Each year, the DRE at my home parish hosted an elaborate Christmas dinner for volunteers and their spouses. People continued to teach years longer than they had anticipated, in part because they hated the thought of missing out on this annual event.

Provide coffee and cookies at in-services. The occasional evening meeting is somehow much more tolerable when fancy snacks are provided. Begin meetings with a question to encourage conversation: What is the best thing that has happened to you since our last meeting? What have you learned from your students lately? Where did you last see God?

7. Jesus prayed and taught others to pray.

Take time to pray. Take time to read Scripture. Take time for quiet. Incorporate all three into any occasion for gathering your catechists. If possible, gather the catechists before class time for a short prayer. During in-services, and especially at the year's orientation, carefully plan prayer services. You might ask different catechists to prepare the prayer for a meeting or parent session. Send a note to catechists on their birthdays or at other appropriate times, letting them know they are in your prayers. Provide plenty of resources for them to plan prayer services with their own classes.

8. Jesus lived his message.

If you want catechists to be present to their young people, then you need to be present to your catechists. If you want volunteers to be witnesses of their faith, you must share your faith with them. If you want catechists to follow catechetical process in their classrooms, make sure you model that same process when you work with them or with any adults. If you want catechists to believe what they are doing is worthwhile, take every opportunity to show them how much they are valued. If you want people to understand that faith formation/religious education is a lifelong endeavor, keep working at it yourself. If you want people to believe that God is good and just and loving, then live that message so it is visible to those you encounter.

9. Jesus patiently trusted the Holy Spirit.

Just think about it. The apostles walked with Jesus for three years, and yet even after he rose from the dead, they still did not immediately understand him or his message. Fortunately, Jesus was patient. He never gave up, even when discouraged. Jesus believed in his calling and did all he could do, but he knew it was not up to him alone. Jesus was able to let go. He trusted in the Holy Spirit to take over.

Follow Jesus

This same Spirit is in each of us, a gift of our Baptism. The same Spirit is in each catechist. If we hope to give our best to those with whom we work, then we need to follow Jesus. We need to believe in our calling, realizing all is not up to us alone. We need to do all we can, then let go and trust the Spirit.

CHAPTER TWENTY-NINE

Six Tasks for the Catechist

My sister and I spent the better part of a summer cleaning out my dad's house. We emptied closets and cupboards that had not been touched since my mother's death sixteen years earlier. In the process, we discovered all sorts of throwaways, as well as quite a few keepsakes. We found one box of treasures tucked away on a back shelf in the basement—a box full of old kitchen tools and mixing bowls we remembered from my grandmother's house. And we surmised from the dates on the newspapers wrapping them that the box had been packed thirty years earlier when my mother and her sisters were emptying their parents' home. Since then it had been put on the shelf and forgotten. My sister and I continued to divide the treasures, packing them in new boxes that will be opened, we hope, before our own daughters find themselves repeating the ritual.

It is a fairly common practice for me, putting things away for safekeeping, and forgetting all about them. I thought of it recently as I was deciding where to keep my copy of the *General Directory*. What a shame it would be if after weeks of studying and discussing the document, I simply tucked it away for safekeeping. Instead, I decided to take it from its shelf and try to unpack at least one small section: the fundamental tasks of catechesis (see *GDC* #84-87).

Probably my favorite sentence in the document is the opening statement in paragraph 80 (from *Catechesi Tradendae* 5): "The definitive aim of catechesis is to put people not only in touch, but in communion and intimacy, with Jesus Christ." The *Directory* goes on to explain that catechesis realizes this objective through six "diverse, interrelated tasks" (*GDC* #85-86), which are named and described in the paragraphs that follow.

These tasks are the work of the whole community, applicable to adults and children alike, but for now I plan to focus on catechists who work with children.

I will look at each task and offer basic suggestions on how to help realize them. As you read, remember what the *Directory* has to say about catechizing children and young people who are still in the process of initiation (who have not yet received Eucharist or Confirmation). Paragraph 67, for example, says that initiatory catechesis should be comprehensive and systematic, an apprenticeship of Christian life, surpassing merely the instructional. Initiatory catechesis centers on "what constitutes the nucleus of Christian experience, the most fundamental certainties of the faith and the most essential evangelical values" (*GDC* #67). Keeping all this in mind, let us look at the six fundamental tasks of catechesis.

1. Promote knowledge of the faith.

Handing on the words and stories that allow others to explain their faith to the world is the first task of catechesis. The catechist's job is helping people come to a gradual knowledge of the whole faith, introducing it, then encouraging them to deepen their understanding of both Scripture and Tradition. In working with children, the emphasis is on "gradual." Since young people still involved in the process of initiation only need to know the most fundamental certainties of the faith, keep this in mind when planning classes or activities and when choosing a textbook series.

I have listed several ways that a volunteer catechist can help children learn the faith.

- Look over the scope and sequence of the textbook series you are using to get a sense of what you are responsible for teaching and how it fits into the larger picture.

- Read the lesson's objective and skim the lesson plan early so that you have time to think about how you might want to incorporate your own ideas and stories.

- Come prepared, read the teacher's notes and, if necessary, ask your director for outside resources.

- Get to know the strengths and weaknesses of your young people so that you can plan accordingly.

- Vary your approaches, since the attention span of children is limited. Reading, discussing, storytelling, using audiovisuals, interacting, writing, drawing and role playing are only some of the ways to help children.

- Try a change of environment. Leave the desks and tables for carpet space. If the weather is nice, try moving outside or to another place in the building. (Remember to let your director know if you are leaving your classroom.) A different location can leave an impression on young people and make for a more memorable learning experience.

- Make eye contact. This is one way of ascertaining whether youngsters are paying attention and listening. It is also an excellent way of giving them individual recognition.

- Be mindful of their age and abilities, keeping lessons, examples and stories appropriate to their level. They have years ahead of them to learn about their faith. You do not have to teach them everything.

2. Provide liturgical education.

This task includes and then goes beyond teaching *about* the liturgy and the sacraments; catechists are expected to help others to become more attuned to a *liturgical life*. They do this by helping people to grow in prayer, encouraging attitudes of thanksgiving and repentance, instilling confidence in prayer and promoting community spirit. Liturgical education recognizes that living in communion with Christ leads to a celebration of his presence in the Church's sacraments, especially the Eucharist.

Catechists can begin to introduce children to the liturgical life of the Church in subtle ways. Consider whether some of the following ideas could be used in your parish.

- Begin and end each session with the same ritual: Lay out a cloth, light a candle, read from Scripture, say a prayer.

- Establish other rituals during your time together. We are a Church of rituals and children have a built-in need for the comfort they offer. All rituals need not be religious. Show and tell, bringing a picture from home, singing a song followed by break time—all can become rituals, contributing to a child's sense of belonging and well-being.

- Recognize the liturgical seasons by using the appropriate seasonal color for the cloth you use during prayer time, the paper you draw or write on or as a bulletin board background.

- Celebrate the liturgical seasons and Church holy days at the appropriate times: Advent during Advent, Christmas at Christmas, Lent at Lent and all fifty days of Easter.

- Introduce some of the prayers and songs from the liturgy, simple responses for younger children and longer prayers and songs for older children.

- Read the Sunday readings with older children or introduce the scriptural theme to younger ones.

- Tour the church, answering any questions the children might have. Teach them the appropriate words for what they see and ask about.

- Plan reconciliation services as well as liturgies together as a group. You might invite another group of children to join you or ask their parents to attend.

3. Give moral formation.

Catechists must help others become aware of their responsibilities as disciples. To believe in Jesus demands a commitment "to think like him, to judge like him and to live as he lived" (GDC #53). It involves a "journey of interior transformation" (GDC #85). Catechists also help others become aware of the social consequences of following the gospel demands. In our time with children, we should mirror Christian life, our words and actions modeling what we teach.

Decide with your young people some basic rules of order that will help maintain respect for yourself and others.

Encourage sharing possessions as well as information; work cooperatively rather than competitively.

Teach different ways of handling conflict. Allow young people to resolve their problems and encourage them to use words to express their feelings.

Model honesty by sharing your own feelings. Let children know when you are tired, angry, frustrated.

Apply each lesson to the children's everyday life and give them time to brainstorm ways they can live out what you have talked about.

4. Teach children to pray.

Catechists must teach others to pray as Jesus prayed. That includes teaching rote prayers, particularly the Our Father, encouraging children to pray from the heart in their own words, teaching them to rest in silence, meditating and finding God in the quiet of contemplative prayer. We are to teach them the habit of prayer that Jesus practiced, always offering thanksgiving and praise to the Father, our creator.

Lead children in a simple rote prayer. Begin or end sessions with the same prayer until all of the children know it from memory.

Talk about the meaning of a familiar prayer. Ask children to write the prayer in their own words.

Vary prayer types. Encourage youngsters to give praise and thanksgiving, ask for forgiveness and offer petitions.

Introduce a variety of prayer styles. Lead children in simple meditations: For older children, try journaling; for younger children, try prayer drawings.

Include some quiet each time you meet. In this age of constant sound, quiet is an important experience to introduce to young people.

5. Educate children for community life.

Catechists ought to impress on others an understanding and experience of Christian community. The *Directory* repeatedly refers to catechesis as an apprenticeship of faith lived out *in community* and says that every dimension of catechesis must be rooted in human experience. We are asked to remember the gospel's call for attitudes of simplicity, humility, solicitude with others, care for the alienated, fraternal correction and mutual forgiveness. Catechists must work to build community among the children in their care. Parish directors also need to work with catechists to discover ways to help children connect with the larger parish community and the community outside the parish.

Begin the year by getting to know each other. Before opening any books or teaching any lessons, try to establish an atmosphere of trust.

Reserve time during each session for activities that help young people to get to know each other.

Listen, listen, listen. Give young people an opportunity to talk about what is happening in their lives. By giving young people an opportunity to reflect on their experiences, we are introducing them to the valuable lifelong skill of theological reflection.

Make sure everyone is treated equally; do not tolerate anyone's laughing at or belittling another. Encourage the young people themselves to expect this type of behavior.

Bring in some simple treats to share (check this out with the parish director first), explaining that table fellowship was an essential part of Jesus' ministry.

Plan time together outside the regular session. Arrange a prayer service, a fun outing or a service project that will bring youngsters together. (Be sure to get the permission of the director as well as all the necessary permission slips from parents.)

6. Initiate into mission.

The final task spelled out in the *Directory* asks catechists to challenge others to assume their role as missionaries, proclaiming their faith through word and action: "The evangelical attitudes which Jesus taught his disciples when he sent them on mission are precisely those which catechesis must nourish: to seek out the lost sheep, proclaim and heal at the same time, to be poor, without money or knapsack; to place one's trust in the Father and in the support of the Holy Spirit; to expect no other reward than the joy of working for the Kingdom…" (*GDC* #86).

Missionary activity is the natural outgrowth of an alive faith. Even small children can express their faith by reaching out to the world around them. Parish programs should help catechists incorporate this task into their regular yearly planning. Below are suggestions for introducing young people to the idea of mission.

Decide with your young people on different ways to help those in need. Look within the parish, making cards for homebound or welcome signs for the newly baptized. Look outside the parish for service opportunities—tray favors for a children's hospital or cookies for a shelter.

Contact the person in charge of parish outreach to ask if there are projects in which your young people can work together with the larger parish community.

Encourage youngsters to talk about their faith with each other and their parents. Send home simple discussion starters or projects that can be carried out by families.

Put together an all-star scrapbook of recognized saints and everyday people who live out the missionary spirit.

Summing Up

Although I have focused on catechists and children, it would be difficult to overstress that catechesis is the work of the whole Church. Each of the six tasks outlined here applies to parents as well as the community as catechists. Both parents and parish (as a whole) must live out each of these tasks if they are to grow in their own faith and pass it on to their children.

When my sister and I looked into that old box in my parents' basement, we had no idea what some of the kitchen tools were used for. How much nicer it would have been if they had been taken out and their purpose had been explained. When treasures are unpacked and used, they become even more valuable to the next generation. The *General Directory* is like that. It offers all sorts of valuable catechetical lessons to help us grow in faith as individuals and as a Church.

Index

conversion
    catechesis as process of
        ongoing, 11-12
    and evangelization, 5
    and objective of catechesis, 8
    and returned Catholics, 158,
        161
    of those with superficial faith,
        6-7
coordinator role of catechetical
    leaders, 20, 181-182
Creed, Apostles', 84, 117
cultural environment
    assessing parish location, 14
    family exposure to religion,
        187-188
    holistic approach to catechesis,
        35
    support for individual faith,
        44

daily life, faith in, 73
Darcy-Berube, Françoise, 31, 33,
    174-175
deed as vehicle of evangelization,
    5
developmentally disabled
    children, programs for, 151-
    156
diocesan media center, 28
director of religious education
    catechist training role, 201
    challenge to be catechetical
        leaders, 17-20
    and communion with Jesus
        goal of catechesis, 23
    evolution of position, 179-180
    and new focus of catechesis,
        11-12
    as professional educators, 169
    and Reconciliation, 101, 102

and use of parochial school
    facilities, 53
See also leadership
*Directory for Masses with Children,
    The (DMC)*, 80-81
disabled children, programs for,
    151-156
discipleship
    and adult catechesis, 129
    as basic vocabulary element,
        68
    defining, 12-13
    and gospel message
        effectiveness, 14-15
    Jesus' example, 36
    and personal empowerment,
        74
    programs for returned
        Catholics, 160-161
    youth programs, 135
divine pedagogy, 22
Divine Revelation, 5
See also God

Easter Vigil, 117
educator role of catechetical
    leaders
    and alternative models of
        education, 18
    community as catechist, 49-54
    and goals of catechesis, 22
    service activities, 55-58
    types of parish programs, 43-
        48
    See also director of religious
        education; liturgy
elders concept, 176-178
empowerment, faith as, 73-74
entertainment, videos as source of
    wholesome, 26

219